CAPTAIN'S LOG

CAPTAIN'S LOG

Airline Pilot Adventures

Captain Lovell Wright

Text layout and cover design by Jonathan Gullery

ISBN: 978-1-7336292-0-1

Printed in the United States of America

Contents

National Airline

Unemployment

Career Airline

On the Jump Seat

This book is dedicated to my wife, Kathy, and all my amazing children. They deserve the highest quality work I could produce. In many ways this is their story also.

Acknowledgements

This project has taken years of personal effort. Writing these stories, however, was a labor of love for me. Not so much for all the other details! I am grateful for the dozens of people who have helped me put it all together. I could not have done it without them.

My wife, Kathy, has given as much as anyone with her support and help, and putting up with me throughout this process. My children were fountains of such great ideas when we brainstormed together.

My mother will probably never know the extent of her influence on all of my writing. She was my first teacher, and the quality of my writing is largely a product of the many hours she spent tutoring me in my youth. She was the first to proof read this manuscript and offer suggestions for improvement. Thanks, Mom.

Rachel Farnsworth, The Stay At Home Chef, and her husband, Stephen were so gracious and helpful with hints for publishing success.

The late LeRoy Skidmore was instrumental in my early success as an aviator. There was a point when he had taught me everything I knew. Unfortunately he passed away long before the fruit of his efforts matured for me. I have to thank my life-long friend Wayne Lyman for his role in piquing my early interest in aviation and pointing me in LeRoy's direction.

I owe a great deal of my success to all of my instructors and fellow pilots who have made me a better airman and helped me enjoy the process as well. I can say the same for the flight attendants with whom I have worked. So many of them have taught me and made my airline career more enjoyable.

While I enjoyed writing this book, I wasn't sure if anyone would enjoy reading it. Thanks to those who took the time to read it and provide valuable feedback, especially Marcie Cozzens, Kirk and Paula Watkins, Penny Robertson and Steve Castillo.

Thanks to Xiao Palmer for her comprehensive editorial analysis. This book is better as a result of her effort. James Luen was so gracious and helpful in sharing his expertise with computer-generated illustrations. I also greatly appreciate the artistic touch that Aimee Potts added to this work. Her illustrations enriched the overall quality of the project.

A big thank you to Jonathan Gullery for his work on the layout and cover design. He took my simple work and transformed it into something amazing. I am so grateful for his talent, expertise and patience throughout the proofing process.

Thank you all for helping me to make this work possible.

Author's Note

All of the stories included in this book are my personal experiences over the course of decades of flying experience. I continue to fly for a major US airline and I have a responsibility to maintain my anonymity for my own sake and for the sake of my company. While all of the stories you are about to read are true, many of the names have been changed to protect the individuals. I have also withheld and/or changed specific airline and airport names to the same end. Sometimes the changes are obvious; sometimes they are not. I have no intent to impugn or embarrass anyone.

I have learned so many lessons throughout my career. I continue to learn everyday and I hope to never stop learning. Some have suggested that I have been too honest in describing some of my learning experiences, to the point of embarrassing myself. While I admit there are things I wish I had done differently, I believe the lessons that experience has taught me offer a great deal of value to those who want to learn from my mistakes.

For those who simply want enjoyment and entertainment, I believe you will find it in the stories that follow. Writing out my experiences has been a labor of love and I have thoroughly enjoyed it. I have been a part of so many interesting tales that I find it all rather amazing as I have looked back. I hope you will too.

Introduction

I love my job! It's the best part-time job in the world! It's been called "living the dream." I travel all over the United States and across borders and oceans to international destinations. I visit interesting places, see interesting sights and meet interesting people. Day after day, I fly big jets equipped with remarkable technology that safely and reliably whisk us from "here to there." I do what many people dream of doing; what most consider mysterious and amazing.

I still find it thrilling and fun, most of the time. Some days I walk to my aircraft feeling "the need for speed." While many might take the technological miracle of flight for granted, seeing it as mundane and routine, I still feel the magic as I careen down the runway and lift hundreds of thousands of pounds into the air. I also still enjoy watching other airplanes do the same. I still bask in the wonder of soaring through the sky at hundreds of miles per hour in a pressurized tube, miles above the earth. It amazes me that humans are uninvited guests in the atmosphere, yet Mother Nature generally tolerates us being there anyway.

My office is a bit small, but the view is incredible! Oh, the sights that I've seen! The view from above can be awe-inspiring. Watching an electrical storm up close and personal is amazing. You haven't lived until you've approached a cloud at over 500 mph and punched through like a bullet through a target; or climbed through a cloud layer and then skimmed along the top at that speed. I've seen sun dogs, Saint Elmo's fire and brilliant northern lights. It's breathtaking at times.

Of course, my job isn't nonstop enjoyment. Some days are challenging, some are tedious and some downright annoying. Sometimes patience wears thin. Nobody likes mechanical breakdowns, weather delays, security issues, etc. When a flight is delayed the crew is generally working for free. A flight attendant once shared with me her secret to a great attitude, "I come to work every day expecting to be three hours late. So when we're not, it's a good day." Most of the time (about 90% for me personally) we are on time and the customers are happy.

I am so grateful for the opportunity I have to be where I'm at. I've achieved what relatively few have done. The pilot fraternity/sorority is somewhat small. Most of us have paid a significant price in effort, dollars, blood, sweat and tears. Climbing the mountain has been difficult, sometimes facing pitfalls that made me question whether I could ever make it. Even looking back, I'm sometimes amazed that I made it. I believe a divine hand has helped many times. I am blessed! It is most definitely not *easy* to get here—nothing worthwhile or rewarding ever is—but I *will* say that it's worth it and the current outlook for an airline pilot career is rather rosy. The worldwide airline industry is in desperate need of qualified airline pilots and the supply is dwindling which makes us a very valuable resource for the foreseeable future.

Even considering all the great things I've mentioned, it's ultimately about the people I have worked with along the way. Working with good people makes the long days not so long and the hard days not so hard. I've made life-long friends and learned so much from so many people. I don't mean just pilots but also flight attendants, mechanics, dispatchers, instructors, ground support and others. So many people have enriched my experience, made me a better person and helped me smile and laugh along the way.

Once again, I love my job! In the pages that follow I'll share some of the stories and lessons I've learned from more than 30 years of flying from "here to there." Come along and I'll show you the airline world from behind the mysterious flight deck door, through the eyes of a veteran captain.

Student Pilot

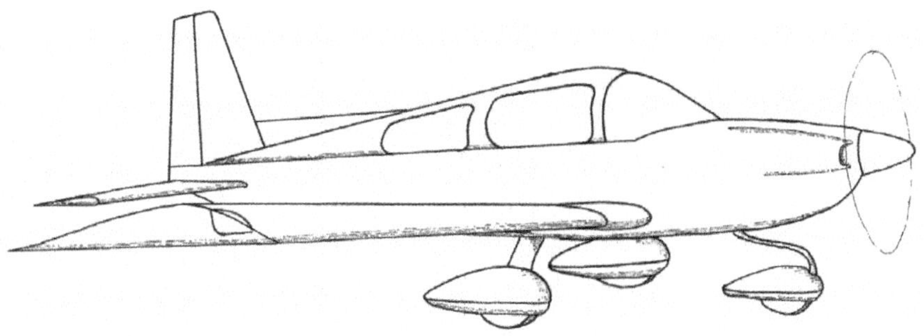

I grew up on a farm where I learned so many valuable life lessons, but none of them would have pointed me to an airline career. I have often wondered at the unlikelihood of me ending up where I am. Nobody in my immediate family was involved in aviation and it's not something I would have imagined except for my friend, Wayne. I met Wayne in grade school and we spent a lot of time together as children. His neighbor, LeRoy, was a private pilot and a high-school teacher. It was LeRoy who began to open my eyes to my potential in the world of aviation when I was in high school.

LeRoy had created a three-year program that led his students to pilot certification upon completion. I didn't realize at the time what a unique and amazing achievement this was at a public high school. I took the introductory course and I was hooked. His program prepared me for the private pilot written exam which I aced my senior year and then I was on my own to transition from the theoretical world of ground training to the practical world of flight training.

FUN FACT

The Federal Aviation Administration (FAA) issues airman certificates, not licenses. This means the agency certifies a pilot as proficient. It does not grant a license, or privilege. This distinction is important in defining the relationship between pilots and the FAA.

As a naive teenager with no idea what to look for in a flight school and no guidance I still somehow ended up in a good place with a good instructor. I spent the next several months learning everything I could from my flight instructor. Training to become a private pilot can be completed in just a few weeks but my experience took almost a year because I was a seventeen-year-old kid with no money. I would work all week after school to get enough money to fly on Saturday. Sometimes it took two weeks. The process stretched all the way into the next fall which meant I had to drive home from college on the weekends. I was eighteen when I earned my private pilot certification.

After that I only flew occasionally with friends and family, logging just a handful of hours over several months. Then I left the country for two years to serve as a missionary in Colombia. It was only after I returned home that I decided to earnestly pursue an airline career. The years that followed became an amazing journey of learning and discovery about a wide range of subjects. I achieved each level of certification that would lead me to an airline captain's seat, but the lessons I learned about life and leadership were even more valuable. My learning odyssey continues to this day and I hope I never stop learning new things.

Captain's Log, Airdate 010822

Wrestling Alligators

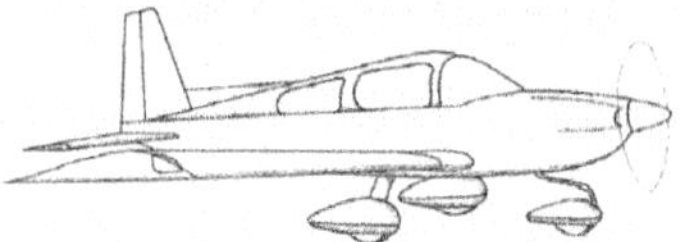

Aircraft: AA5A Grumman Cheetah
Crew: Solo

I was a student pilot on final approach to Salt Lake City (SLC) and I was about to learn one of the most important lessons of my career.

As a seventeen-year-old farm boy, flight training was something completely new and unfamiliar for me. Most of what I knew about airplanes was from a book so I was intimidated at first. My experience with farm equipment was helpful in many ways, but lifting an airplane off the ground and keeping it in the air was new and somewhat mysterious to me at the time. In the air I felt constant stress, never sure if I was one false move away from sudden death. I would often squeeze my hands on the controls in a white-knuckled death grip and my instructor would remind me not to strangle them. This isn't unusual for new trainees with no experience. Flying is really not a natural state for humans so confidence in the air must be learned and earned.

Confidence is a strange and misunderstood thing. It can be easy to confuse confidence with arrogance. These are two extremely different human characteristics. In the pilot's seat, confidence is essential; arrogance is dangerous. Acting confidently is the opposite of being timid or unsure and it's generally reached through experience—you've been there, done that. Flight training should be designed to provide the experience that creates confidence in the machine and your ability, as a pilot, to make it do what you want it to do. While confidence is extremely important, a pilot should never forget to approach what we do with a humble attitude. False bravado is very counterproductive on so many levels. Mother Nature tends to take note of arrogant pilots and frequently finds a way to humble them, sometimes tragically.

This solo flight was just to the local area for practice maneuvers, but the wind was tossing me and the little Cheetah around like a rag doll. As I lined up with the runway for landing, the gusting wind pushed me into a precarious position, but I forced it back where I wanted it. A light bulb suddenly came on in my mind! ***I*** was in control of this machine! From that moment going forward, my flying experience was different. I knew that I was in control and the fear of sudden destruction was being steadily replaced by calm confidence with each successive flight.

This confidence is so important as an airline captain. I assumed it was a prerequisite. Years later, when I began my airline career, I was surprised to find there were pilots who were afraid to fly. They represent an extremely small percentage of the airline world, but these poor pilots sometimes let their airplanes push them around and it's disconcerting to fly with them. While I'm careful not to disrespect the risks involved, I know how my airplane works and how to *make* it do what I want it to do. There are times when it can be like wrestling an alligator—but I *will* whip it into submission.

Captain's Log, Airdate 010902

Emergency!

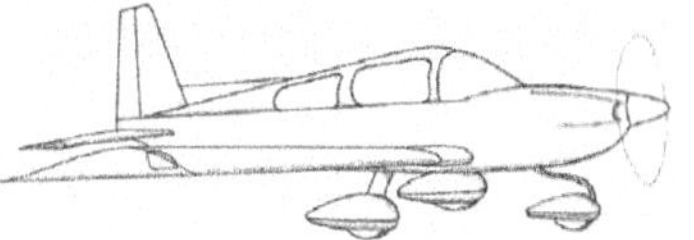

Aircraft: PA38 Piper Tomahawk
Crew: Solo

I had gone to college in Rexburg, Idaho before I could finish my flight training so I had to improvise to find a way to finish my certification requirements. I checked at the local airport and they had a Piper Tomahawk that I could rent very cheaply. I had the local instructor check me out in this new-to-me airplane so I could use it to finish my solo cross-country requirements. At this point, I encountered a fun coincidence in the form of another airplane they had for rental: the sister ship to the Grumman Cheetah I had been flying in Salt Lake City, Utah (SLC). Their registration numbers were almost identical (N9827U & N9887U). When this new instructor checked my logbook, he was as surprised as I was to see the strange coincidence. He explained to me that they had once owned the other airplane but had been forced to sell it years earlier.

My plan for the solo cross-country flight was to fly to Idaho Falls, Idaho (IDA), do a touch-and-go (see definition), then on to Pocatello, Idaho (PIH) with the final leg back to Rexburg (RXE). This would give me just enough hours to fill the requirements. I took off and quickly covered the short distance to IDA. After lining up for the approach, the tower cleared me for a touch-and-go. I began slowing down and extending the flaps for landing, but something unexpected happened—a loud banging noise from the tail of the airplane. My first reaction was fear. I had no idea what had happened and I didn't know if something important might be falling apart. After the initial shock, however, my ingrained instinct was to fly the airplane and calmly assess the situation. The airplane was still flying and still under control. If I could keep it that way for just a minute or two, I would be on the ground.

DEFINITION

Touch-and-Go: A practice landing that is done by briefly touching down and immediately taking off again.

I advised the tower and asked to change my clearance to a full-stop landing. I mentioned the word "emergency" without really appreciating what I had just done. The controller changed my clearance to a full stop and then asked me if I needed the fire trucks to come out to the runway. That suggestion surprised me. I declined and explained that I just needed to stop to find out what was making the noise. In hindsight, I should have accepted the offer. I didn't know what the problem was and having the emergency equipment on hand would have been some good insurance, just in case. It also would have been a unique sight to see a fire truck follow a Piper Tomahawk to the ramp.

I landed and taxied to the parking area where I shut down the engine so I could get out to inspect the airplane. A thin piece of rubber stripping which seals the small gap between the vertical tail and the fuselage had come loose on one end. It had been flopping around in the airstream and slapping the tail in the process. In the air it had sounded much worse than a piece of rubber. I tucked the stripping back in place and made sure everything was legit before continuing on my way. Another learning experience was in the book.

Flight Instructor

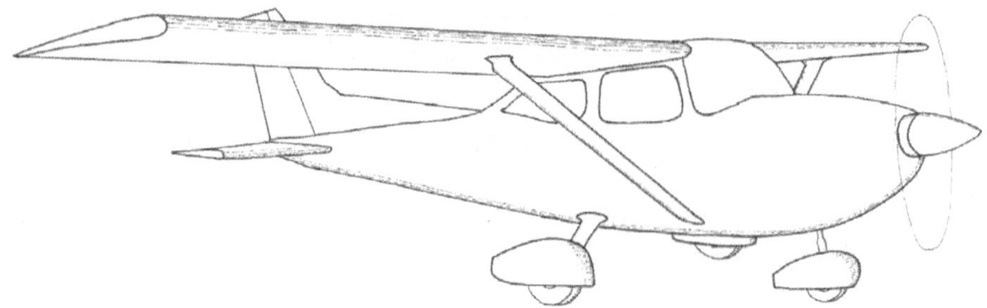

I enjoy teaching. I get a great deal of satisfaction from seeing the light come on when someone "gets it." It's enjoyable to help students understand foundational principles that form the basis for why we do certain things. I would love to continue to give some flight instruction outside the airline world, but the current regulatory structure discourages it because that time counts against our legal flight time limits. This is a mistake that I believe should be addressed in order to facilitate the flow of collective wisdom from so many seasoned airmen to a new generation of pilots.

Working as a flight instructor is typically the first flying job for many professional pilots. It's an opportunity to hone the skills they've developed to that point by teaching others how to do the same. Furthermore, continued learning and expanding those skills is a necessity to be an effective teacher. There's nothing quite like seeing your own students achieve the milestone of their first solo flight. It's amazing and intense—very intense—as you step out of the airplane and watch them take off and land on their own. Nobody gets rich as a flight instructor, but when it's treated as a labor of love, there is so much to be gained from it.

It took several years for me to complete my degree program and flight training certifications. At the end of the process, I was officially a Certified Flight Instructor-Instrument (CFII). Unfortunately, there were not a lot of jobs available at the time because the industry had stagnated somewhat. After graduation, I looked for many months without success. With a wife and three young children to support I started working, out of necessity, at a family-owned rock crushing operation at a quarry east of Las Vegas, Nevada. It was difficult work in the oppressive heat of the Mohave Desert, but it paid the bills. As months went by, however, genuine concern began to build. I was afraid that my pilot career might be teetering on the edge of oblivion.

Our prayers were answered when I found myself in just the right place at just the right time to have a job fall into my lap at North Las Vegas Airport (VGT). Working around my schedule at the quarry, I took an afternoon off to visit flight schools in the Las Vegas area. I had been a CFII for two years, but that certification was about to expire, so I was looking for a good flight school where I could renew my certificate.

One of the places I investigated had an acutely pressing need for instructors that particular day. My value for them was also at a premium because I was certified to teach instrument flying (a different level of skill that must be mastered to fly and navigate solely by reference to instruments). I also happened to be acquainted with one of their instructors from a college class we had taken together. I barely remembered her and I didn't know if she remembered me which I made clear to the instructor evaluating me. Their desperation for new instructors, however, somehow transformed that acquaintance in his mind into us being old college buddies. In the end, I squeaked in the back door and my professional pilot career was underway.

FUN FACT

Pilot certificates do not expire. Flight Instructor certificates are separate documents that do expire, requiring recertification every two years.

My thirteen-month stint working as a full-time flight instructor was an adventure and a challenge. It was only a short time but I look back on it with good memories. I learned a lot and made some great friends. Gen (the aforementioned college buddy) and I ended up working together for many years at three different companies. Another good friend that I met there was Mike. We worked together for four years at two different companies before he ended up at a major US airline. Today we both fly the same airplane (at different carriers) and we talk and text on a regular basis.

Captain's Log, Airdate 070113

Control Freak

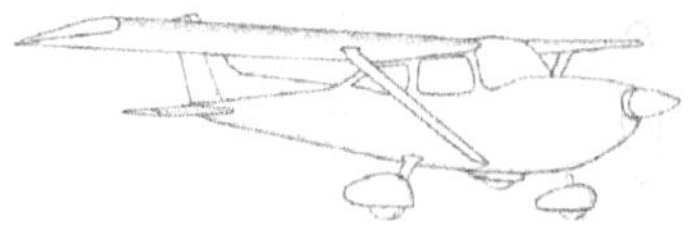

Aircraft: C-172 Cessna Skyhawk

Instructor: Christine

The training and induction process at the flight school involved getting checked out in *their* airplanes and *their* procedures with one of *their* instructors. I had a memorable experience on my second flight. There were a few airplanes in the traffic pattern that morning as we pulled up to the runway hold-short line (see definition). I called the tower to indicate we were ready for takeoff and made note of the aircraft on final approach. The controller responded with, "Cleared for takeoff, no delay." I was uncomfortable with the spacing between myself and the landing airplane, so I indicated we would wait for him to land. The controller freaked out for some reason and told me to taxi clear of the hold-short line and not call him back until I was, "READY. FOR. TAKEOFF."

DEFINITION

Hold-Short Line:
A set of lines painted on the taxiway (see Illustration) indicating where to stop in order to ensure a safe distance from the runway edge.

Hold Short Lines. These yellow lines are painted on the taxiway to indicate where to hold short of the runway.

I had never experienced such a lack of professionalism from Air Traffic Control (ATC) before then and I still haven't to this day. I guess he was having a bad day. Most controllers are helpful and courteous while providing a valuable service, so this was a definite exception.

I don't even like the term "controller" despite its accepted use. I think a more appropriate term would be Air Traffic *Advisor* which more clearly describes the service they provide. The ultimate authority for the safe conduct of any flight rests with the Pilot In Command (PIC). No PIC should ever look for permission from a controller to do what is safe and smart. Controllers in the United States issue *clearances* based on the information they have that the PIC does not (as in, the way is *clear* for you to proceed). Their instructions are not *authorizations* (as in, I grant you permission). It can be a fine line that may seem like splitting hairs and controllers might disagree, but tragedies have occurred as a result of a PIC surrendering his/her authority to a controller who is sitting in a building far from the accident sight.

Captain's Log, Airdate 070118

Enough Room?

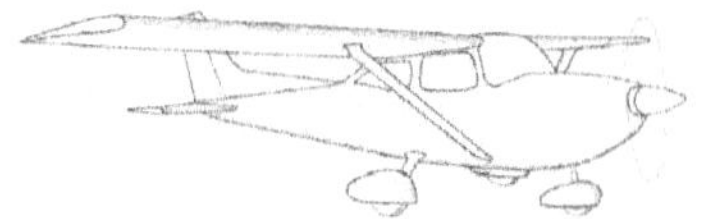

Aircraft: C-172 Cessna Skyhawk

Student: Jon

Flight instructors frequently have the opportunity to accompany a fresh, new trainee on an introductory flight. These are always interesting, as everything is new and unfamiliar for this person you've only just barely met. The typical protocol is to introduce the aircraft and then take it out for about a half hour, to give the newbie an opportunity to "fly" the airplane for several minutes. For initial training, the trainee sits in the pilot's (left) seat with the instructor in the right seat. Most airplanes (and all trainers) have dual controls, so the instructor is always in command regardless of who is moving the controls at any given moment.

The first time I flew with Jon was just such an introductory flight. I made all of the customary instructional points and we hopped into the Cessna 172 for a quick trip. North Las Vegas, Nevada (VGT) had only two runways at the time and they crossed each other. The wind was favoring Runway 12, so I taxied across the end of Runway 7 and held short of Runway 12, awaiting a take-off clearance. As we waited, Jon asked if there was enough room to take off. I reassured him that there was plenty of room. It didn't take long for him to ask again if there was enough room. Considering that he might see something I didn't, I looked carefully to my right along the length of the runway and again reassured him that the runway was clear and much longer than what our little Cessna needed.

The third time took a little longer, but Jon eventually queried again to see if I was *really* sure there was enough room. This time I turned to my left to look at him and discovered his wide-eyed concern about the building directly in front of us on the other side of the runway. Without understanding we were going to make a right turn onto the runway in order to take off, he was rightly expressing his doubt about the space in front of us being enough room for the aircraft to get airborne. I chuckled to myself about the misunderstanding and directed his eyes down the runway to show him there was indeed plenty of room to take off in *that* direction.

FUN FACT

Runways are numbered based on their magnetic heading after dropping the last digit. Runway 12, for example, is aligned with a heading of approximately 120 degrees.

Captain's Log, Airdate 070528

Daddy's Boys

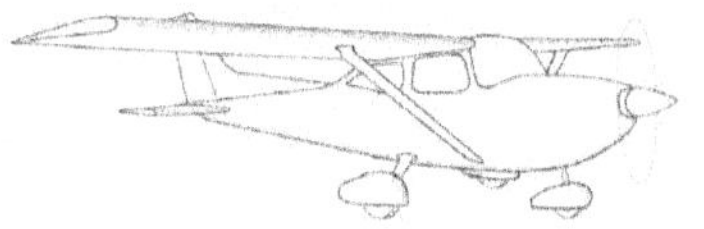

Aircraft: C-172 Cessna Skyhawk

Crew: My three sons

One of the flight school's Cessna 172s had suffered a mechanical failure and had to land at the nearest airport, located in Overton, Nevada (U08). Mechanics were sent to fix the airplane, then a pilot was needed to bring it back to North Las Vegas, Nevada (VGT). I happened to live near Overton so I volunteered for the short recovery flight. I called my wife to explain the situation and see if it was possible for her to meet me in Overton with our three young boys. They were ages five, four and two at the time. One of my favorite things to say to her was, "Trust me," and in this case she did.

I know. What guy in his right mind would take three small boys in a small airplane by himself? Maybe I wasn't in my right mind, but my boys were well-disciplined, it was a short flight and there were car seats involved. It turned out to be a memorable experience for each of them and for me. They loved the flight and the chance to "work" with their dad. I enjoyed having them with me. I even took the opportunity to give them a little flight instruction along the way.

Captain's Log, Airdate 070730

Losing My Lunch

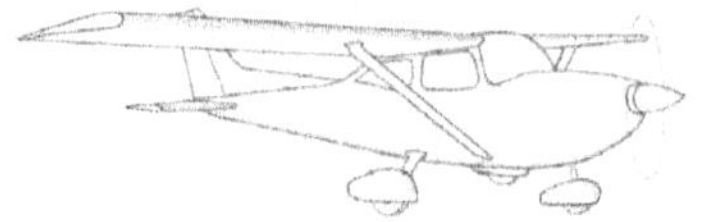

Aircraft: C-152 Cessna Sparrow Hawk

After working as a flight instructor for several months at North Las Vegas, Nevada (VGT), I was getting frustrated with the slow pace at which my hours were accumulating and the meager size of my pay checks. In search of a better opportunity, I applied for a position with my alma mater. I was invited to interview at Embry-Riddle Aeronautical University in Prescott, Arizona (PRC).

I decided to fly to the interview so I rented an old C-152, which is a pretty solid workhorse as a cheap trainer but a very small airplane. It was just right for my solo trip to PRC. As a starving flight instructor, cheap was important, so I had packed a sandwich and some snacks for the day which I placed on the seat next to me.

I took off that morning from VGT and began the slow climb over the Las Vegas Valley. The standard departure path included an initial course to the southwest and then a turn back to the east. As I made the turn, the door opposite me popped open. I instantly snapped my hand over to grab my sandwich but only got one finger on the plastic bag as it slipped out the door. I had just broken a regulation! I worried for a few minutes that it might have hit someone. Eventually I conjured up the idea that a desperately hungry person might have been praying for food at the moment and a sandwich fell from heaven into his lap.

Ultimately, I did not get the "better" job I was seeking that day but something unexpected and even better was on the horizon.

Captain's Log, Airdate 070800

Ecuador To the Rescue

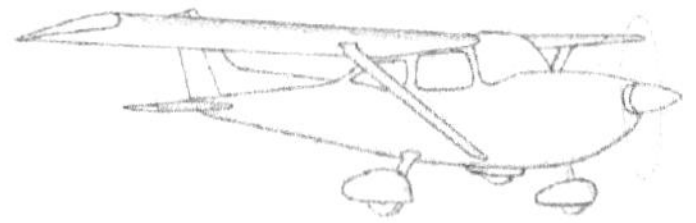

Location: Flight School

Disappointment and frustration were the result of my search for a better opportunity and I was getting concerned about my lack of career progress. I continued to work diligently as a flight instructor, which was really enjoyable but the poverty wages made it unsustainable for the long term. The blessing for which I had been hoping and praying walked into the flight school one day. His name was Bob and he was the director of training for Scenic Airlines which was headquartered across the street at North Las Vegas Airport (VGT). He came in that day looking for a Spanish-speaking instructor to help with a training contract.

I was proficient in speaking Spanish because of a two-year period I spent in Colombia serving as a missionary. Giving two years of my life was a sacrifice that I gladly made, but it came with a price. The airline world is all about seniority. Getting a spot on the seniority list with a good airline is a primary career objective. The sooner this is accomplished, the better. The resulting benefits include better pay, job security, captain upgrade opportunities and overall quality of life as the years go by. With this in mind, any delay can be costly. I believe this confluence of events was a merciful blessing that came just when I needed it *and* was prepared for it.

Scenic was one of the world's largest operators of Twin Otter airplanes, which are great for Grand Canyon air tours. In order to facilitate their training needs, they had built a Twin Otter simulator—a rare resource in the training world. This little gem brought the Ecuadorian Air Force to VGT to complete their annual recurrent training requirements. They were using a small fleet of Twin Otters for transport to and from jungle landing strips. The result of all this for me was an opportunity to sit in on their training and provide translation when needed.

I cannot overstate how important this opportunity was. A desperately needed career path was now opening up for me. I spent two seasons helping with the contract and getting to know many interesting officers in the Ecuadorian Air Force. It was fascinating and educational. After the first season, Bob was impressed with me and he became instrumental in securing for me a pilot position with Scenic Airlines, despite my significant lack of experience.

Local Airline

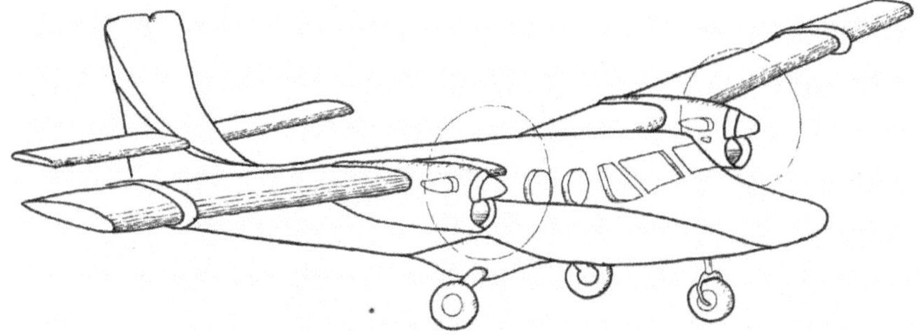

My short career as a full-time flight instructor was over and my adventure in the airline world had begun. Scenic Airlines was the leader in Grand Canyon tours. The DHC-6 DeHavilland Twin Otter is a great airplane for air tours and a lot of fun to fly. It's powered by two ultra-reliable turboprop engines and its wings are designed for high lift at low speeds. The original owner of Scenic also secured certification to enlarge the windows for better sight-seeing and gave the airplane a new name: "Vistaliner." Scenic was the perfect opportunity for me to step up to a higher-performance airplane and begin learning about airline operations. It was also my introduction to the crew environment and I learned so many valuable lessons from good captains and first officers.

Stepping up from single-engine Cessnas to Twin Otters was a bit of a challenge and my previous experience with the Ecuadorian Air Force crews proved a blessing. I had already learned a lot from sitting in on ground school and simulator sessions with them. Of course, it was different when I was the trainee. Getting used to simulator training is a bit of an art form. These machines are meant to replicate the real world and they are very valuable for emergency training. Certain emergency situations like engine fires, hydraulic failures, etc. are obviously problematic to try to replicate in a real airplane. While the training value of simulators is very useful, they're not quite the same as the real thing. It takes some getting used to. One of the keys to success is focusing on a very disciplined scan of the instruments because any other environmental feedback (sights, sounds, feel) may or may not prove useful. It can be more like playing a video game than flying an airplane.

The other step up was to the crew environment. The human element in the flight deck presents its own challenges and there are many principles to be learned. Airlines have been focused for decades on a concept called Crew Resource Management (CRM). CRM encompasses many aspects including crew interactions. In many ways the dynamics between crew members is a microcosm of society. A multitude of lessons about flying—and life in general—are available if it is approached as a learning laboratory.

Most captains are good and others not so much. The wide spectrum of difference between captains creates an interesting dilemma. It has been said that the hardest job in aviation is that of first officer (FO). The FO is expected to know everything, be able to do everything and held responsible for most everything, but doesn't get the same pay, respect or credit as a captain. Also, adjusting to each captain, like a chameleon, can sometimes be a challenge. It's an important skill to learn the right balance between supporting the captain but knowing when to assertively offer a different point of view when the situation calls for it.

DEFINITION

First Officer: The Second in Command (sometimes called a copilot) who sits in the right seat and usually alternates flying duties with the captain.

I flew with one particularly unpleasant captain I will call "Bill." Bill had some insecurities that twisted his ability to work effectively with other crew members. He had a tendency to belittle first officers to compensate. He harassed me a lot and once told me I was the worst pilot at the company. Sometimes I wonder if he thought his approach was a helpful training technique, but for me it definitely was not. It would have been great to ignore him but, unfortunately, he was in a position of authority. It seemed he made it his personal mission to make my life miserable.

Jack was another challenging captain. Many FOs refused to fly with him. My first trip with him was strained and quiet. At one point, he was a bit slow changing a radio frequency so, wanting to be helpful, I nonchalantly reached over and poked the button to change it for him. He turned to me with a stoic expression and sternly said, "You know, if there's a job eliminated around here, it won't be mine." Then he turned and looked forward again, as quiet as before. This was my introduction to Jack, but what I learned about him was his need to assert authority. Once he was sure the FO understood he was in charge, he was actually pleasant to work with and I learned a lot from him.

Once I got on Jack's good side, he frequently shared useful tips with me. One valuable point was about simplified troubleshooting of jet engines. They need three things: fuel flow, ignition and airflow (rotation). If an engine fails it's probably due to a lack of one of these and if you can restore what's missing, it will probably restart. Another tip: when facing an emergency, be aware of your position relative to the airport and don't get too far away. Yet another pearl: don't do the same thing to both engines at the same time. He once shared a simple rule about emergencies. He asked what the first action should be in any abnormal situation. I was thinking "fly the airplane" or "aviate, navigate, communicate." He said you look at the FO and ask, "What the hell did you do?" That was Jack's sense of humor. I think.

Scenic also provided air transportation for Grand Canyon river runners. One particular challenge was a landing strip called Bar Ten Ranch. It is situated about half-way between the two ends of the canyon just above the edge of the steep inner gorge but below the outer canyon rim. It's a great location to pick up and drop off river adventurists. It's also a notably short, narrow, dirt strip in a very remote area. The approach to Bar Ten went over a large lava flow just before touching down on a strip with a relatively steep upslope. This combination, along with the "rising" canyon walls, created illusions that demanded a high level of focus and sound technique to ensure a correct touchdown and stop before the end of the dirt runway. The surrounding terrain had a tendency to produce unpredictable wind patterns as well. It was a handful.

Flying air tours was a lot of fun. Operating over Grand Canyon itself was heavily regulated. The routes and altitudes were prescribed. But once we left the limits of the designated airspace we were free to make up our own routes. There was some freedom to explore. One interesting site was the ancient cliff dwelling ruins in Northern Arizona. These were a favorite to get a look at on the way to Monument Valley in Southern Utah. Another favorite was the canyons, lakes and ghost town between Bryce Canyon, Utah (BCE) and Grand Canyon, Arizona (GCN).

I will always look back with fondness on the time I spent flying Twin Otters for Scenic Airlines. It was enjoyable and educational. I worked with a lot of good people. I'm so glad there's a large section in my logbook with those memories.

Captain's Log, Airdate 080000

Learning from Veterans

Aircraft: DHC-6 Twin Otter

Crew: Captain Art

Captain Mike

While there are some difficult captains, most are good at what they do. One of the great blessings afforded me at Scenic Airlines was flying with seasoned airline captains. These veteran airmen were forced to retire at age 60 (per regulatory requirement) after long, successful airline careers but returned to the flight deck for various reasons. It was a pleasure to fly with them and an opportunity to learn so much from their experience.

Two of these were Art (retired, Trans World Airlines) and Mike (retired, Pacific Southwest Airlines). These two loved to fly. They worked part-time at Scenic and did other flying on the side, such as ferrying Twin Otters across the Pacific Ocean. Even after decades of flying, these two loved to sit behind the yoke (see definition). These ferry missions were 14-hour flights with no autopilot. The length of the flight required a conversion of the passenger cabin into an extra, makeshift "fuel tank" composed of 55-gallon drums connected to the main fuel tank with a network of hoses. This unique situation called for grossly overweight takeoffs. I once asked Art about it, "What happens if you lose an engine on takeoff?" He replied with mock reverence, "We go out in a blaze of glory!"

Mike had one of the most cheerful attitudes I've ever come across. He also shared with me some of his adventures in repossessing aircraft—stories of sneaking onto airports in the middle of the night to "steal" airplanes. He was also a member of the Screen Actors Guild and flew in numerous movie scenes. He once shared a story with me from his time as an instructor in the U.S. Navy during World War II. While doing maneuvers, His airplane got into a flat spin. This is a very dangerous situation from which recovery is unlikely. This particular flight demon was portrayed in the movie *Top Gun* and led to Goose's death as he and Maverick ejected from their doomed aircraft. Mike and his student faced a similar choice. The student climbed out of the trainer and sailed away on a parachute. At that point something strange happened. The student's exit had changed the plane's weight and center of gravity. Mike was about to follow but the nose dropped slightly. Seeing an opportunity to save the aircraft, he climbed back in the cockpit. He rocked the nose up and down enough to create sufficient airflow over the wings and then recovered from the spin. He said the student never forgave him.

DEFINITION

Yoke (or control yoke): The primary flight control. It is used to pitch up and down and bank left and right. It looks like a partial steering wheel.

Mike gave me one of the greatest gifts of my early career. When it came time for me to upgrade to captain, I was passed over because a check airman had spread negative reports about me. To counter this I began asking every Captain at the company for feedback. Nearly everyone was very positive. When I asked Mike, his thoughtful response was this, "You are an *airman*. You have the instincts of an *airman*. You would be surprised how many pilots just don't have that." While I already felt confident as a pilot, this assessment from a seasoned veteran was an endorsement that I needed at the time and made a difference for me going forward.

Captain's Log, Airdate 080000

Logging Lessons

Aircraft: DHC-6 Twin Otter

The quest to earn my fourth stripe (captains wear four stripes, first officers wear three) nudged me into a very educational and enlightening phase of professional development. In order to ensure I was learning and growing as much as I could, I implemented two strategies: logging "lessons learned" and tallying daily mistakes.

Each day I made sure I logged at least one important lesson I learned that day. This forced me to look harder at myself, my captains and our operational environment to find a valuable educational nugget.

I also kept track of the mistakes I made each day. Everyone brace yourself for a major spoiler alert! Airline pilots make mistakes on a regular basis. Many would say there's no such thing as a perfect flight. Of course, the vast majority of these errors are simple and relatively harmless. Virtually every pilot understands what the critical, unacceptable mistakes are and guards rather vigilantly against them. What I learned was that keeping a tally of mistakes each day led me to maintain a focus on perfection. Initially there were a lot of errors, but the total steadily decreased to the point that I occasionally achieved the goal of no identifiable mistakes on a given day.

Captain's Log, Airdate 080000

A Tale of Two Incidents

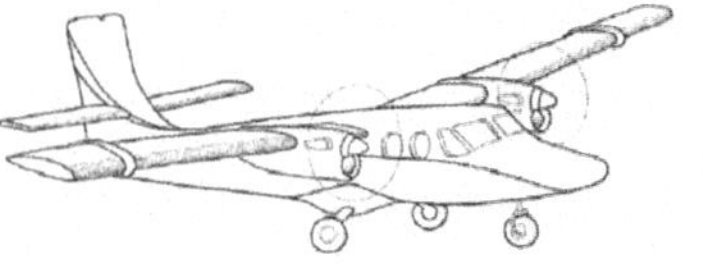

Aircraft: DHC-6 Twin Otter

Scenic presented opportunities for rather varied operational environments. We offered daily flights to Monument Valley (UT25) in Southern Utah. This remote airport serves the local Native-American Tribe and sightseers who want to visit the amazing, natural rock formations nearby. It consists of just one short, narrow, mostly dirt landing strip with an even shorter paved section at the end. Normally we always try to land and take off into the wind, but the cliffs surrounding this airport require one way in (towards the cliffs) and one way out (away from the cliffs), regardless of the wind direction. The nature of this terrain also created other challenging wind conditions. In order to mitigate these wind-related risks, our policy was to divert to nearby Kayenta, Arizona (OV7) when the wind reached a predetermined limit.

Monument Valley set the stage for one of the most valuable lessons I learned at Scenic: *honesty in flying is essential.* I have referred to this lesson in training situations numerous times since then. This narrow landing strip was a notorious challenge and it occasionally claimed victims in the form of incident reports placed on a pilot's record. Two of these incidents happened almost back-to-back and created a remarkable illustration contrasting what to do and *what not to do*. While neither of the two incidents involved me directly I was well acquainted with those involved and the details about what happened. I will call the two crews "A" and "B".

Crew A began their takeoff and encountered a nasty wind shear before liftoff that pushed them off the runway. The captain made a decision to continue anyway and the result was a very rough, bouncing excursion through the uneven desert terrain before lift off. The captain then decided to continue to Grand Canyon, Arizona (GCN). After landing there, he called the chief pilot and reported the excursion, but downplayed the severity and indicated no damage to the aircraft. He then continued to North Las Vegas, Nevada (VGT). The next day the aircraft flew again before mechanics began noticing anomalies during a routine inspection. This led to further inspections which ultimately revealed some extensive damage to the aircraft, most significant of which was broken engine mounts. It was only by the grace of God that the engine did not separate from the aircraft. Crew A had placed a lot of people at substantial risk in an effort to hide their mistake.

The incident with crew B occurred just a few days later, before anybody really knew the extent of what had happened with crew A. Crew B's takeoff scenario was nearly identical to the first incident but with a crucial difference—the captain decided to abort the takeoff once the wind shear had pushed them off the runway. The result was very different in that the nose wheel got caught abruptly on a berm and the aircraft tipped forward, coming to rest on the nose and the right wing tip. No one was significantly injured, but the aircraft suffered substantial damage. Technicians had to remove the wings and then haul the pieces out on a truck.

Several days later, investigators showed up to examine what had happened to crew B. They soon discovered a set of tire tracks that revealed the excursion of aircraft A was much worse than what had been reported. When confronted with the mounting evidence of what had happened, crew A made the mistake of insisting their original story was true. They got fired! The FAA got involved and revoked the captain's certificates. The captain's original decision to continue the takeoff was wrong, but still defensible. The string of decisions that followed, attempting to cover up the truth, was reckless, dangerous and inexcusable. Crew B was given some additional training and they promptly returned to flying status. Despite the severity of the damage to their aircraft, crew B came clean about everything that happened and subsequently avoided any further consequences.

The moral of the story is that we all have an obligation to each other to be honest. Hiding potential aircraft damage is a breach of trust between fellow crew members and the traveling public. It simply cannot be tolerated.

Captain's Log, Airdate 080519

An Ounce of Seatbelt Keeps Pounds Secure

Aircraft: DHC-6 Twin Otter

Crew: Captain John

John was a little bit quirky but he had a lot of experience and a really good understanding of the Twin Otter and our operational complexities. I always enjoyed flying with him. The day's assignment was to take a tour group to Monument Valley (UT25) but the wind was too strong and gusty, so we switched to Kayenta, Arizona (OV7) as plan B. It was close by and usually subject to the same wind conditions, but the runway and the surrounding terrain were more favorable to deal with the wind.

We approached Kayenta from the south, descending along the edge of the nearby mesa. As we did so, a dramatic and invisible hazard lay ahead. The wind coming off the edge of the mesa had developed a strong, rotating vortex. Suddenly, the aircraft was thrown wildly and banked hard to the left. I glanced at the control yoke and saw John had it fully turned the other direction, with little effect. Everything in the cabin that was not firmly secured was thrown every which way. The passengers screamed! The upset lasted only a brief moment before John quickly restored control. Then, in the midst of this very tense situation, John held up the demo seat belt with his free hand for everyone to see and calmly made the following announcement, "That's why we wear seat belts." What an understatement! I couldn't help but smile and chuckle to myself.

Captain's Log, Airdate 080727

Watching My Six

Aircraft: DHC-6 Twin Otter
Crew: Captain Bill

It was my birthday. It should have been a good day, but I got sucked into a terrible situation that jeopardized my career. After finishing late the night before, I was asked to participate in a "training" flight the next morning. The rest period in between would not have been legal for a revenue flight (a flight with paying passengers), but training flights don't have the same restrictions. The company was facing a difficult situation and there was pressure for everyone to help out.

DEFINITION

Check Ride:
A pass-fail flight test taken regularly to verify a pilot is current and proficient.

The situation had arisen from an unusual set of circumstances. The FAA had notified the airline that first officers were required to do some extra training and they were only allowed a short window for completion. Scenic always did its flight training in the wee hours of the morning due to airspace restrictions during normal business hours at Las Vegas, Nevada (LAS). Despite less than two hours of rest, I was prevailed upon to participate and assured it was only a training flight, *not a check ride*. Even worse, Bill was the instructor conducting the training. Strangely enough, with no time to prepare and minimal rest, I didn't do well. Bill decided I had failed the "training flight."

So because I was willing to help out, I got caught in a bad situation. Eventually it worked out but the lesson I learned that day was to make sure I was looking out for myself (watching my six, in pilot speak). Helping out is good, but not if it comes with too much personal risk. It's okay to say no. If rest is insufficient for a revenue flight, it's not enough for a training flight either.

FUN FACT

Looking outside an airplane, the sky is divided into sections based on a clock face. Twelve o'clock is straight ahead and Six o'clock is directly behind.

Captain's Log, Airdate 081105

Frozen Finger Challenge

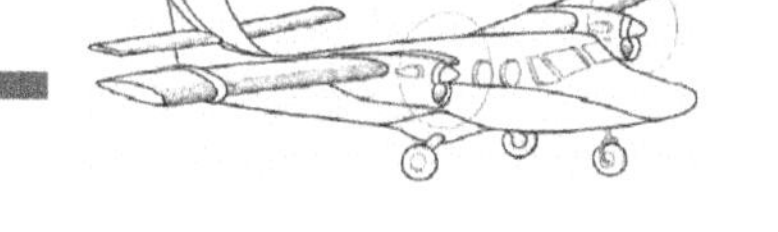

Aircraft: DHC-6 Twin Otter

Crew: Captain Jason

Scenic had two separate branches: the main operation was based in Las Vegas and included the Twin Otters. The other was a single-engine Cessna group based in Page, Arizona (PGA). At one point the CEO made a trip to PGA and spoke to the employees about seasonal cuts meant to trim the "deadwood." His remarks went over like a lead balloon. The pilots there took particular offense to the term and began calling themselves the "Deadwood Squadron." The group included a lot of good pilots who were good to work with.

(#1) Twin Otter Eyeball Window (inside). These windows are used for airflow in the flight deck. When rotated forward, airflow is directed in. When rotated to the back, airflow is pulled out. (#2) Twin Otter Eyeball Window (outside). These windows could be opened or closed and adjusted any direction.

Jason was part of the Deadwoods and I enjoyed flying with him, but he was a bit off-the-wall. On this cold November morning, we encountered some icing conditions and Jason suggested a contest to see who could leave their fingers out in the freezing air the longest. The Twin Otter has four-inch "eyeball" windows (see illustrations) on each side of the flight deck that pop out and rotate—to the front to scoop fresh air in, or to the back to suction air out. It's just big enough to stick a couple fingers out into the airstream. The challenge was to see who could leave their fingers out in the freezing air the longest. We both squirmed and gritted our teeth through the battle of wills, but after a couple minutes Jason finally gave up and cried, "This is stupid!" While I certainly could not disagree, I had claimed the victory so I pulled my frozen fingers back inside for some rehab.

Captain's Log, Airdate 090104

Naked and Afraid

Aircraft: DHC-6 Twin Otter

Crew: Captain Jack

After a year at Scenic I was feeling pretty comfortable, maybe too comfortable. I had come to the point that I enjoyed flying with Jack and he seemed to feel the same way. On this beautiful day, however, our complacency produced a simple mistake that turned into a much bigger problem.

We had departed from a remote airport headed for Las Vegas, Nevada (LAS). When we reached the designated point outside the LAS airspace we checked in like any other day. The controller said, "Radar contact, cleared into the class B airspace, direct Sam's Town, left base 19 right." This was a standard clearance that these guys would rattle off dozens of times each day for tour operators returning from east of LAS. The translation: "I have you on my radar display. You're cleared to enter my airspace. Fly directly to Sam's Town (a distinctive local landmark) for an approach to Runway 19 Right."

I knew exactly what he had said because I always made a habit of *ensuring* I heard the required phrases before entering the class B airspace (the busy airspace that surrounds major airports).

We made our way toward the airport, but things got interesting when it came time to switch our radio to the tower frequency. We asked if we should switch and the controller's response was, "Scenic 37, where are you?" That's *the last thing* any pilot wants to hear in the middle of busy airspace. It's like that nightmare where you show up for school or work and realize you're naked.

The problem was that our transponder was not switched on. Somehow this got overlooked at the beginning of the flight and continued unnoticed because we had not been in controlled airspace. A transponder allows an aircraft to be easily identified and tracked by Air Traffic Control. The controller, a victim of his own complacency, had erroneously "identified" us on initial contact and issued a clearance into his airspace without actually seeing us on his display. It took several minutes for us to cross his busy airspace and, without our information on his radar screen, he forgot we were there.

A tense situation ensued for a few moments as he vectored us around to fit us back into the sequence of arrivals but eventually it ended up working out okay. It turned out to be a "no harm, no foul" scenario because the controller knew he shared the blame. From my side of it, there were two important lessons: first, always beware of complacency and, second, always maintain checklist discipline. Checklists are invaluable tools, but only if they are used correctly. The endless repetition of checklists and the rhythmic challenge-response cadence can lull crew members into mindlessly responding to an item without actually checking it. The transponder should have been on per the checklist, but we missed it. Beware of responding without doing.

Captain's Log, Airdate 090211

Who Has the Controls?

Aircraft: DHC-6 Twin Otter

Crew: Captain Bill

It was always a challenge to fly with Bill, but today was especially difficult. The schedule was to fly to Grand Canyon, Arizona (GCN), on to Monument Valley (UT25) and then the reverse—four legs total. He assigned me to fly the first leg. There was a significant crosswind at Las Vegas, Nevada (LAS) that morning and he didn't like how much control correction I had used on takeoff. I explained my reasoning, but he insisted I was wrong.

After landing at GCN we followed the normal routine for the two-hour break and went to lunch. With the hours that had passed, I had forgotten about the crosswind issue but on the next leg Bill decided to teach me a lesson. Without any indication of his intentions, he made the next take off with his arms folded on his chest. This, of course, was surprising and unnerving as we accelerated down the runway with nobody manning the controls. I asked if he had it and he indicated yes, but still left his arms folded. I asked again and he barked at me. As we reached rotation speed, he quickly took the controls and lifted the aircraft off the runway.

I was utterly stunned by the whole sequence and was trying to process what had just happened as we ascended into the sky above GCN. When he finally spoke, he snapped at me for failing to make my standard call outs during the takeoff run. Again, I was stunned—and angry. He then proceeded to explain his "valuable" lesson to me that crosswind control corrections were unnecessary. Once more, I was stunned—and even more angry. The Twin Otter can be a bit squirrelly on the ground and it is actually very important to apply a crosswind correction. Not only was he wrong, but he had chosen a terribly foolish way to make his point. The rest of the day became a process of managing my anger so it wouldn't become a threat to the success of the remaining flights. It was a challenge, but I forced myself to remain focused on what needed to be done rather than get caught up in the hostile atmosphere.

Captain's Log, Airdate 090304

Preterm Labor

Aircraft: DHC-6 Twin Otter
Crew: Captain Jane

As I logged more experience, I developed a calm, quiet confidence. Some captains are more excitable, like Jane. The day was fairly mundane and boring which is a good thing for airline flying. Outside the operation, however, a potential distraction was brewing. The flight to Grand Canyon, Arizona (GCN) that morning was uneventful and the return to North Las Vegas, Nevada (VGT) was much the same—until dispatch called. They informed us that my wife had been taken to the hospital with pre-term labor. More than two months remained before my daughter was due, so this was rather worrisome.

Jane got really excited about it. While I was definitely concerned, there was nothing I could do about it while I was in the air. The most important priority at the moment was to focus on the successful completion of the flight. Jane kept asking if I was okay; was I going to make it? While the concern was sweet, the demeanor was too excited, almost frantic. It got to the point that I wished they hadn't told us anything until after landing.

Dispatch called a replacement and let me have the rest of the day off to attend to my wife at the hospital. The next month was a challenge—bedrest, in and out of the hospital, never knowing for sure what the outcome would be. Thankfully, our long-anticipated daughter did arrive safe and healthy a few weeks later.

Captain's Log, Airdate 090505

Trust Me, I'm a Captain

Aircraft: DHC-6 Twin Otter
Crew: Check Airman Dick

I've always made a point of being honest with passengers. Some in the airline industry feel a need to lie to them but it doesn't make sense to me. As a result, the traveling public has developed a general skepticism which is amusing most of the time but occasionally aggravating. Such was the case on this trip. It was a typical Grand Canyon/Monument Valley tour. I was flying with Dick that day. He was the check airman overseeing my Initial Operating Experience (IOE) as a captain. The first stop was Grand Canyon, Arizona (GCN) where our travelers took a short tour and then we continued to Monument Valley, Utah (UT25)

We were to take an unusually large group of tourists on this trip. They were accompanied by their own director who took charge of most tour functions. Because of the group size, multiple aircraft were assigned to the trip. The director happened to be on my airplane. The normal itinerary for this trip was to return to GCN after the tour at UT25 in order to refuel for the flight back to Las Vegas, Nevada (LAS). The tour director asked if we could skip the intermediate leg for a non-stop return. I explained to her that I did not have enough fuel for that, so the return to GCN would be necessary. I looked very young at the time and Dick had gray hair so the director assumed he knew more than I did. She asked *him* if a direct flight to LAS was possible. He assured her it was not.

As luck would have it, one of the aircraft in the group only ended up with a half-load of passengers and thus they were able to take enough fuel on the leg to UT25 to allow the non-stop return the director was seeking. She discovered this little tidbit of information during the ground tour. Afterward, she asked again if it was possible, pointing out the plan for the other aircraft. I explained why the other airplane was capable of doing so and assured her that we could not do the same. She was obviously unhappy with my response. We took off for GCN and Dick decided to conduct a certification check on the Grand Canyon "black routes" for me along the way. This involved crisscrossing the canyon at designated points. The training protocol also required that we reference the chart (map) while doing so.

FUN FACT

Anytime a pilot begins flying a new airplane and/or upgrades to captain, a period of IOE under the supervision of a specially-qualified check airman is required.

All of this led to a strange situation upon arrival at GCN. After the passengers had deplaned, the station manager approached us to ask what had gone so wrong. The tour director had gone straight to him to complain about their "terrifying" flight. She blasted us for getting lost and zig-zagging back and forth trying to find where to go on our maps. Apparently, she was still upset about having to return to GCN and wasn't buying the excuse about "not enough fuel." It would have been funny if it hadn't been so annoying.

Captain's Log, Airdate 090507

Quarter of a Landing

Aircraft: DHC-6 Twin Otter

Crew: First Officer Mike

On the first flight I commanded after finishing my supervised Initial Operating Experience (IOE), I was paired with Mike, one of my best friends. We had worked at the same flight school and now we were flying at Scenic together. It was a good day. We took an uneventful trip to Grand Canyon, Arizona (GCN). As we began the descent and arrival for landing, I gave Mike a typical briefing for the approach. He then pulled a quarter out of his pocket and placed it on one of the fire handles (see illustration). He looked at me seriously and threw down the gauntlet, "That quarter better not fall off on landing." The challenge was on.

Twin Otter Fire Handles and Engine Instruments. There's just enough room on the fire handle to put a quarter on it but any bumps or vibration would knock it off.

It was a nice, smooth day at GCN, so there were no excuses. I focused intently on smooth control with each successive extension of the flaps. As the airplane neared the ground, I smoothly flared into the landing all the way to a gentle kiss onto the runway. The quarter stayed put and a grin spread across my face. At that point the challenge was met, so I twisted the power levers into reverse. This, of course, produced the typical vibration and the quarter fell. He laughed. Now, if I would have known the deceleration was included in the challenge, I would have gently eased into the brakes without reversing the propellers. After all these years, we still disagree about this.

Captain's Log, Airdate 091111

Minding the Tiller

Aircraft: DHC-6 Twin Otter
Crew: First Officer Devin

It was another beautiful day at the Canyon and I was about to make one of the biggest mistakes of my career. I had taken the leg to Grand Canyon, Arizona (GCN) and Devin was flying back to North Las Vegas, Nevada (VGT). I enjoyed working with him and today was no different. This flight was an empty leg to return to VGT for a new group of passengers. Devin gently lifted the aircraft off the runway and we were on our way.

About fifteen minutes after takeoff, we started to notice an unusual vibration. It got progressively worse, so we began troubleshooting. We discovered through trial and error that feathering one of the propellers (turning the blades to align with the airflow) with the power at idle significantly reduced the vibration. This seemed to me to indicate some kind of imbalance with that propeller. We decided not to shut down the engine because it was still useful, but we left it at idle power to control the vibration. By this time, we were over half way to VGT so we continued and advised dispatch of our condition.

Upon entering the Las Vegas airspace we declared an emergency. Devin was doing a great job and never gave me any reason to doubt his control of the situation, so I decided to let him continue with the approach and landing. We hadn't done anything terribly wrong up to that point, but the big error was about to occur. As we approached the runway, I let the nature of the situation distract me from making sure the landing checklist was done. One critical item on this checklist is to ensure the nose-wheel steering tiller is centered. I failed to check it. The nose wheel was turned about 80° to the left instead of straight ahead.

The whole situation was a result of this one anomaly. The vibration was caused by the uncentered nose wheel disrupting the airflow. The power reduction on one engine and the accompanying control input had resulted in a slip condition (the airplane flying at an angle through the air) that straightened the airflow in relation to the nose wheel, thus reducing the vibration. What we thought was a propeller imbalance was nothing more than the nose wheel turned sideways.

As the nose wheel touched down, the aircraft began to veer to the left. Despite both of us standing on the right brake pedal, it continued left, finally coming to rest with the left main wheel and the nose wheel off the side of the runway. I quickly realized what the problem was, but it was too late. Ultimately, nothing on the airplane or the airport was damaged, but our egos and reputations had taken a hit. I straightened the nose wheel and we taxied to the terminal.

We were removed from the schedule and sequestered for a

debrief. I knew what the problem had been and I knew it was my fault. I explained this to the chief pilot but, for some reason, they insisted on hanging most of the blame on Devin because he was at the controls. I still don't fully understand why they chose that course of action. ***I*** was the captain and it was ***my*** fault but they still sent him for remedial training while I was returned to the schedule that same day.

FUN FACT

Complex airplanes have controllable propellers. The blade angle is manipulated by the pilot to meet the airflow at different angles: negative for reverse thrust, flat for high power settings and perpendicular (called the feathered position) for no power. This could be compared to different gears in a car.

Whatever their reasoning, I felt awful. Devin was taking the hit for my mistake. I learned some important lessons that day: 1) when facing an unfamiliar condition, reach out on the radio for as much help as possible, 2) don't let *anything* distract from critical tasks, and 3) the captain should take the controls in an emergency unless there is a compelling reason to do otherwise. If I had been at the controls, I probably could not have stopped the runway excursion but maybe Devin might have been less distracted than I had been. Of course, that's Monday-morning-quarterback speculation. At least the blame would not all have been dumped on my friend, Devin.

Captain's Log, Airdate 091215

Oil Caps Gone Wild

Aircraft: DHC-6 Twin Otter

Crew: First Officer Steve

Winter was the slow season for Scenic. It was a time to catch up on things like painting aircraft. For some strange reason I never understood, management chose a paint shop in Mena, Arkansas (MEZ). A crew would fly the plane there and return on another airline to Las Vegas, Nevada (LAS). The closest available airline service was in Little Rock, Arkansas (LIT) which was a two-hour drive from MEZ. When the paint job was finished another crew would do the same thing in reverse or fly the next airplane out there to exchange for the first.

It was my turn to take this cushy assignment with Steve and another crew, to pick up two aircraft and fly them back. Everything started normally and it was fun to have the other crew to talk with on the radio for the long flight. We had to stop in Amarillo, Texas (AMA) to refuel, so we all decided it would be a good idea to check the oil in our engines. This is normally a maintenance function, but we didn't have any mechanics available, so we did it ourselves. Finding the oil levels normal, we continued our trip. Not long after takeoff, the first officer of the other aircraft reported to us on the radio that they were losing oil pressure in one of their engines. I told him that wasn't something to joke about. He wasn't!

Soon thereafter, they declared an emergency and returned to AMA. The other captain had failed to properly secure the oil cap after checking the oil level and they were forced to shut down that engine. Fortunately, it was only one engine. A decision was made for us to stay with them, so we followed them right back to AMA. The expelled oil had made quite a mess and it turned out we had to spend the night there before we could continue.

That captain was a guy who liked to poke fun at me in the wake of my incident with the steering tiller from the previous month. Steve, my first officer, suggested it was now my turn to harass him for *his* bonehead mistake. Considering he was already embarrassed enough, I decided to let it go. Even so, he didn't harass me so much after that. I suppose he learned a lesson about karma that night. On a positive note, the next day we met some space shuttle pilots while waiting at the airport and enjoyed talking with them about what it's like to fly that amazing machine.

Captain's Log, Airdate 100223

It's Just Easier to Go VFR

Aircraft: DHC-6 Twin Otter

Crew: First Officer Steve

While tours were our main business at Scenic, we also served the occasional charter customer. One memorable charter was to the copper mines in Central Arizona. Three aircraft were assigned to this trip, which was to take some regular tourists to Grand Canyon, Arizona (GCN) then reposition from there to Scottsdale, Arizona (SDL) to pick up the charter customers. Another anomaly that day was bad weather. Nearly all of our flying was in visual conditions. There was obviously less tourist appeal if they couldn't see Grand Canyon and its surrounding wonders. In these cases, it was up to the customer if they wanted to forego the air tour and just fly directly to GCN for a ground tour.

The overcast weather required operation under Instrument Flight Rules (IFR). IFR is the set of flight rules that must be observed when pilots can't see the ground or other airplanes because of clouds, fog, haze or other obscuring phenomena. IFR relieves certain responsibilities from the flight crew (who can't see anything outside) and places them with Air Traffic Control. These rules are very different from Visual Flight Rules (VFR) which place almost all of the responsibility for airspace, navigation and terrain/collision avoidance with the pilots.

We flew under IFR to GCN that morning and the decision to continue IFR to SDL seemed like a no-brainer. We were shocked to discover after arriving at GCN that the other two captains, who had arrived before us, had already convinced the dispatcher that IFR was not necessary. They wanted to fly VFR. Steve and I were incredulous and we asked the other two captains why they would do that when the conditions were so marginal. Their response was, "It's just easier to go VFR." This statement is simply ridiculous. While it might be easier for the dispatcher to plan the flight VFR, it's certainly not easier to operate it that way. In fact, the opposite is true. VFR leaves everything on the pilots' shoulders.

FUN FACT

Instrument Flight Rules (IFR) vs Visual Flight Rules (VFR) is a critical distinction. IFR is generally the safer option and all flights above 18,000 feet are required to operate under IFR.

VFR rules would likely make it necessary to do some "scud running" (picking our way between or under clouds). A wise aviator once described this foolish practice as "attempting to maintain visual contact with the terrain without making physical contact." The wise thing to do would have been to wish them good luck and simply opt out of their madness. Unfortunately, I felt trapped by their decision because the lead captain was Bill. He was an assistant chief pilot and I was afraid he would make me regret going against his decision. As it was, we went along with their plan and I regretted it anyway. In fact, after all these years, I *still* regret it. But even though I was willing to accept the attempt, we remained determined that if anything looked too risky, we would simply obtain an IFR clearance and climb up into the clouds for the remainder of the flight.

Fortunately, the flight to SDL did not become unacceptably risky, but was fraught with all kinds of difficulties. Each time we encountered a problem, we would look at each other and sarcastically say, "It's just easier to go VFR." Steve is still a friend of mine. Even with the many years that have passed, I can bump into him today, repeat that phrase and still have a good laugh with him about that nonsense.

National Airline

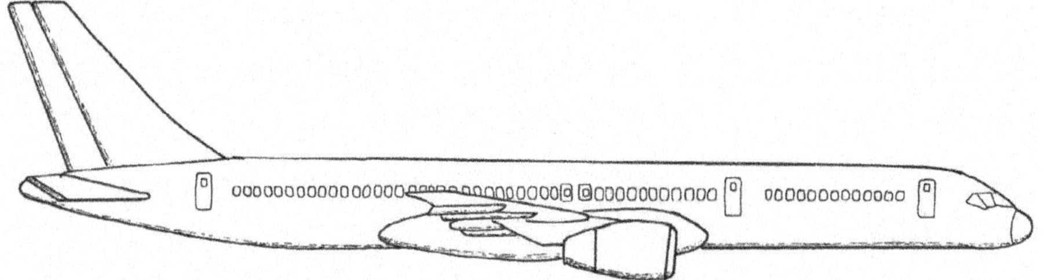

Once again, I was in the right place at the right time to take advantage of a great opportunity. National Airlines was a start-up company based in Las Vegas, Nevada flying Boeing 757s to major metropolitan airports across the United States. I really had no business aspiring to make the jump from Scenic to National. The next logical step for me was to advance to a regional airline for a couple years. Most of my colleagues who were single (including my good friend, Mike) did just that after one or two seasons at Scenic, but I couldn't see how I could support my family on regional airline pay, so I stayed there for three and a half years.

I can only thank God once again for preparing a pathway for me. Mike (different Mike) was one of my favorite captains at Scenic. He also had a family and faced the same dilemma, so he decided to take a non-pilot job at National, which was growing quickly. By the summer of that year he had advanced to a position in the safety department and he agreed to personally present my résumé to the Chief Pilot. I interviewed a short time later and was offered a position on the spot. I was set to take another big step forward.

My career path had made a steep climb from single-engine Cessnas to Twin Otters to Boeing 757s and the learning curve was equally steep. I had learned a lot in a short time and I was about to learn a lot more. Initial training at any airline is frequently described as drinking from a fire hose and the challenge was accentuated for me because of the big jump. There was so much new and unfamiliar stuff for me to absorb about the airplane, the environment and the operation. Fortunately, National had a great training mindset that was perfect for someone willing to learn.

It was my first experience with full-motion simulators. That alone was a challenge for me. These are amazing machines that create such a high-fidelity experience that no training is required in the real airplane. Many people are shocked when I tell them that the first time a new pilot sits at the controls of the real airplane is on a revenue flight with regular passengers. This aspect also caused my mind to develop a strange melding with reality. When I started flying the real airplane it was so much like the simulator that I had to constantly remind myself, "This is real. This is not the simulator."

The Boeing 757 is one of the best transport category airplanes ever built and I loved flying that machine. Many pilots have used the nickname "Slender Lady" because of its long, narrow body (among other features). It's an amazing aircraft that I still rave about to anyone willing to listen. It has lots of power and performance capability, a roomy flight deck with an intuitive pilot interface and impressive technological tools. It is categorized as a "glass" aircraft which indicates a high level of built-in digital technology. Yet, with all of it's capability, it was a dream to fly. Even though it is only a first generation "glass" airplane, I think it's one of Boeing's greatest achievements.

I even loved our call sign, Red Rock. It's still the coolest call sign I've ever used. The only negative aspect about National is that it was too short-lived. I was only there for a year and a half before it went out of business. Due to a short furlough after September 11th, I was only flying for less than 12 months of that time, logging less than 900 hours. It was good while it lasted and it still lives in the hearts of so many of us who worked hard to make it a success. Red Rock is dead! Long live Red Rock!

Captain's Log, Airdate 110817

Energy Management

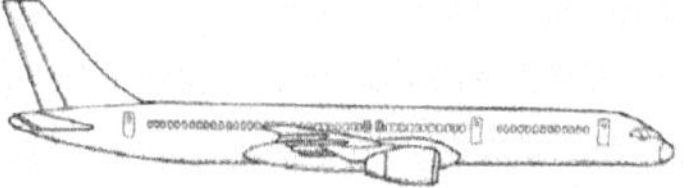

Aircraft: B-757
Crew: Check Airman Tom

The transition from Twin Otter to B-757 was a stretch for me. I didn't have any trouble learning its computerized functions, but it was more complex than anything I had previously flown. Plus, most of the operating environment was new and different. It was also faster and more powerful, which made it difficult for me to keep up. I considered it an accomplishment that I made it through the classroom and simulator training program without any extra training. The next step was Initial Operating Experience (IOE) on the real airplane under the supervision of a check airman.

Tom had a unique personality that annoyed some people—not me. He had the heart and mind of a teacher, which is just what I needed. Regulations require a minimum of 25 hours of IOE but a check airman will not release a new pilot from their supervision until clear and consistent proficiency is demonstrated. At the completion of 25 hours, I was close, but one concept was eluding me: energy management. My previous experience had not required much thought about energy management because the Twin Otter had so much inherent aerodynamic drag it was easy to make it slow down. I was going from one of the dirtiest (aerodynamic speak for lots of drag) airplanes to one of the cleanest. The B-757's ultra-clean aerodynamic design was an important accomplishment for Boeing but a challenge for pilots. That airplane did not like to slow down!

On my first day of IOE the check airman said it was simple. Three-to-one is all I needed to know for descent planning: three miles are needed for every 1000 feet of altitude. If the cruise altitude is 33,000 feet, a distance of 99 miles is needed for the descent. That seemed simple enough, but consistent application was not that simple and I was confused as to why my planning wasn't working out. This was intensely frustrating because I knew how to fly airplanes, but this beast was mocking me and beginning to erode my confidence.

FUN FACT

Anytime a pilot begins flying a new airplane and/or upgrades to captain, a period of IOE under the supervision of a specially-qualified check airman is required.

The schedule for the day was to fly two round trips to the same destination. Tom shared his plan at the beginning of the day: I was going to fly all four legs with his coaching and I would get it by the end of the day. It sounded great to me. I flew the first two legs, but the coaching didn't seem to help. At that point, Tom did something amazing that I hadn't seen before nor have I seen since. I don't know if he made it up on the spot, but it was the perfect training technique for the situation. He explained that he would fly the next leg and he would *think out loud* as he applied simple energy management techniques.

During the next descent the light bulb came on for me! I listened to his thought process of *continuous evaluation of all the pertinent factors* and strategizing from the top of descent all the way to touchdown. I thought to myself, "Ohhhh! That's easy! Why didn't somebody explain that to me before?" It was the magic elixir! I will always be grateful to Tom for his wisdom and insight in finding a way to get me to drink it.

Captain's Log, Airdate 110826

Let's Wait a Minute

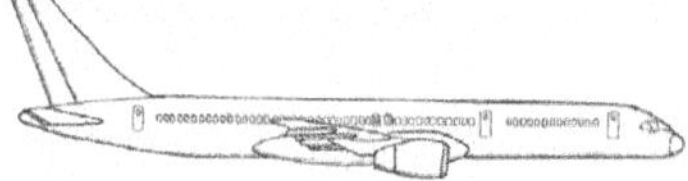

Aircraft: B-757
Crew: Captain Dennis

This was my first flight after completing the Initial Operating Experience (IOE) requirements with a check airman. I was paired with Dennis, an old friend from Scenic, and we were on our way to Chicago, Illinois (ORD). National was a favorite for pilots from other airlines who were using airline jump-seat privileges for travel to or from home. We had two of these pilots in the flight deck with us that day. Las Vegas, Nevada (LAS) was in the throes of another searing summer but our B-757 shrugged off the heat and quickly climbed out of the Valley. As we topped 10,000 feet and began accelerating to a normal climb speed, a caution message appeared indicating an overheat on our right engine.

I began working the checklist which called for Dennis to reduce the thrust on the "hot" engine. An overheat is typically due to a leak of hot air from the engine which can potentially cause a lot of damage. The thrust reduction was aimed at decreasing the hot air leak, but, if it didn't work, the next step was to shut down the engine. *What?* My first post-IOE flight and we were going to *shut down an engine*? Dennis said, "Let's give it a minute." I started the timer. A minute went by and nothing changed, so Dennis called for the shut-down checklist. *This was crazy!* I started to read. Meanwhile, right behind me, one of the jump-seaters had his eyes glued on the display, hoping to make it home without any delays. He was the first to see it and exclaimed, "It went away!" After ensuring we could restore normal thrust without the caution returning, we called dispatch to apprise them of the situation. We agreed on a plan to continue to ORD.

Upon arrival we turned the aircraft over to the mechanics and the next flight crew and we went to the hotel. The following day's schedule would take us back to LAS followed by a quick back-and-forth to San Francisco, California (SFO). Morning came too early and we were back at it. Another day, another airplane. The flight to LAS was uneventful and we loaded up again for SFO. While waiting in line for takeoff, we heard an unusual report on the tower frequency: one of our company flights had declared an emergency and was returning to LAS with an engine shut down. Dennis suggested a bet on whether the emergency aircraft was the same one we had from the day before. We had a perfect view alongside the runway as it landed—N513NA. He was right!

FUN FACT

Jet engines produce hot air and a portion of this hot, pressurized air is bled off the engine. It is called "bleed air" and is used in other systems such as pressurization.

The situation had reinforced an important lesson. It's very important to remember in any emergency that very few things require rushed action. Conversely, most emergency situations can be aggravated by acting too quickly. Haste makes waste, especially in an airplane. Whether this case was an actual hot air leak which had become worse or something more simple, it was about to get fixed. I never heard which it was, but the thing that I will always remember is Dennis calmly suggesting, "Let's give it a minute." At least I wasn't declaring an emergency on my first day.

Captain's Log, Airdate 110911

Shock and Awe!

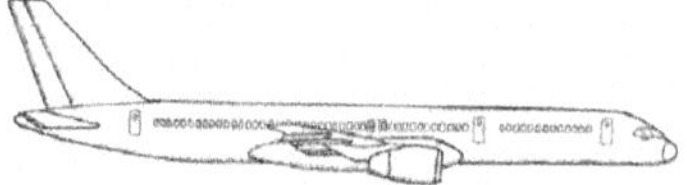

Aircraft: B-757
Crew: Captain John

I was settling in to my new routine with National, criss-crossing the country from sea to shining sea. The previous day was the first time I had met John and our trip had taken us from Las Vegas, Nevada (LAS) to San Francisco, California (SFO) and then on to Chicago, Illinois (ORD), arriving in the wee hours of the morning. I slept in late the next morning because of our late arrival and the need to rest for the next day. The phone woke me up early on Tuesday, September 11, and I answered it despite still being half asleep. It was John. He was telling me something about the World Trade Center and the Pentagon. It didn't make any sense, so I was trying to figure out if he was the practical-joker type as I turned on the TV.

WHAT A SHOCK!

It was mind-numbing as I sat there for hours trying to digest the scenes of devastation in New York, Washington and Pennsylvania. Shock! Tears! Uncertainty! Confusion! Thousands were dead! Tens of thousands were injured and suffering! Millions were grieving and afraid! Our nation was under attack! My wife called to find out if I was okay. New York was one of our busiest stations. In less than a month on line with National, I had already done five "overnights" (typically about 24-36 hours) in Manhattan. I had been walking around Central Park only a few days earlier.

In an unprecedented move, the airspace over the United States had been shut down. This left thousands of airline crews and passengers stuck where they were. Our little crew of seven became somewhat of a family that week. We cried together, laughed together. We ate together and shopped together. We began *healing* together! We rented an SUV and toured Chicago. By the end of the week, we were good friends and the flight attendants bought me a muumuu dress to tease me for my naïveté about what such a thing was.

The whole week had been such a strange and different experience for all of us. We were there until Friday before we were finally allowed to leave for home. As we climbed out of ORD, it felt so nice—therapeutic—to have my hands on the controls of my B-757. I hand-flew it all the way up to cruise altitude before turning on the autopilot.

Upon arrival in LAS I was informed that I would be furloughed (temporarily downsized). National was in bankruptcy prior to this time, but there was now additional uncertainty that came with the new reality settling over the whole airline industry. It forced our management team to make a defensive move to reduce payroll costs, cutting the bottom 10 percent of the pilot seniority list. The good news: it only lasted for two months. The bad news: the time limit had run out on my training before I could log the necessary hours to "consolidate" all that I had learned as a new trainee. Regulation now required that I take a check ride again before I could return to flying. This was an adventure in itself.

Captain's Log, Airdate 111213

Which Engine?

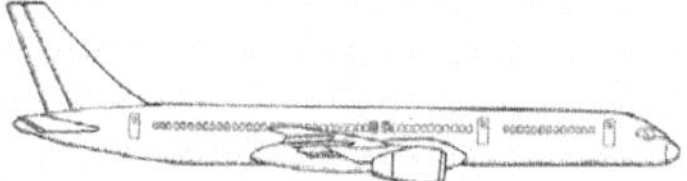

Aircraft: B-757

Crew: Captain Jay

My transition to the B-757 demanded a steep learning curve. After a month of flying the airplane (about 90 hours), I was starting to get ahead of the curve a bit. Regulations impose a requirement for airline pilots who are newly-trained in an aircraft. They must log at least 100 hours in that airplane within a short time frame in order to "consolidate" what has been learned. Unfortunately, the uncertainty stemming from the terrorist attacks on September 11th had caused me to be "furloughed" before I met that requirement. I was off for almost three months. In order to reset my training process, I would need to take a new check ride in a simulator before I could return to flying status.

This would be a challenge for anyone, but it was accentuated for me because of the steep learning curve I was already experiencing and almost three months of no flying. Jay, a regular captain whom I had never met before, would be in the captain's seat for this check ride. For some reason the check airman decided to give me an engine failure on the first takeoff. This sequence was leading towards an almost predictable outcome.

When an engine fails, the remaining engine thrust on the other side creates a rather large imbalance. The pilot's most important action in this situation is to apply rudder control to counteract this thrust imbalance. I did exactly that and lifted the airplane (simulator) safely off the runway. At this point (less than 100 feet off the ground) Jay offered what he considered a helpful observation, "It's the left engine." This was not a standard call and I was not used to hearing it. For whatever reason, my mind interpreted what he said as pointing out that my rudder control was wrong. I reacted by switching my feet on the control pedals. The result was 41,000 pounds of thrust on the right engine driving the airplane to the left and my rudder control helping it that direction. It was stunning how quickly the airplane flipped over and crashed.

There were a lot of lessons to be learned from this situation. In a lot of ways, our training department had created a recipe for failure but the most important lessons I took from this experience were about the importance of communication and the value of standardization. Clear communication is essential in the flight deck. Misunderstandings can sometimes be catastrophic. It's worth the effort to make sure the recipient understands what you intended to communicate. Jay's identification of the failed engine was a non-standard call which produced confusion in my inexperienced mind. Standard call outs are designed to produce clear, concise communication in critical moments and keep everyone on the same page.

In the end, the failure was almost inconsequential. The

company simply gave me some additional training. I passed the ensuing check ride and I was returned to flying status within a few days. I was back in the saddle again.

Captain's Log, Airdate 120214

Riding Through San Francisco

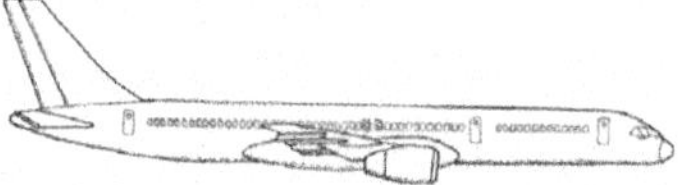

Aircraft: B-757

Crew: Captain Charlie

One of the best parts of my experience with National was long "over-nights" in great places. Our hotel in the City by the Bay was at Fisherman's Wharf which allowed for interesting diversions within walking distance. Pier 39 was a great attraction just a few minutes away. San Francisco's famous up and down city streets made for interesting walks. The Golden Gate Bridge, however, was a little bit too far to walk so I rented a bike.

It was a great day exploring the Bay Area. I rode across the bridge and through the hills on the north side. The bike rental was fairly cheap but the price I paid the next few days was rather painful. I could barely walk and it was only day two of a four-day trip. I winced every time I moved. Charlie, of course, had no compassion for the crazy guy who did this to himself. He laughed at me every time I groaned.

Captain's Log, Airdate 120509

Coffin Corner

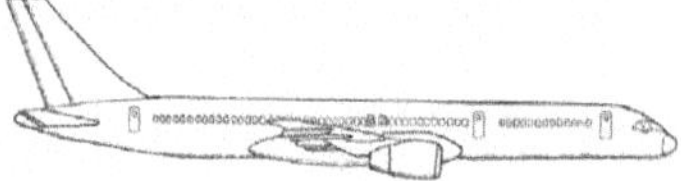

Aircraft: B-757

Crew: Captain Maury

High-altitude aerodynamics is an important area for pilots to learn about and understand. Transport airplanes begin reaching their aerodynamic limits somewhere in the mid to high thirty-thousand-foot range. There is only so much that wings and engines are capable of doing as the air gets too thin. It's vitally important for pilots to respect these limits. The laws of physics make no exceptions for ignorance. The most important factors affecting these limits are air temperature and aircraft weight. Higher temperatures and higher weights mean lower altitude limits. The most critical consideration as the aircraft reaches its limit is the convergence of high-speed and low-speed buffet.

Low-speed buffet is associated with an aerodynamic phenomenon known as a stall. It is caused by the disruption of airflow over the wing when the angle between the wing and the airflow increases to the point where the air no longer flows smoothly over it. The disruption in airflow causes lift to deteriorate and this turbulent flow can be felt inside the airplane. If a wing is allowed to progress into a full stall, the lift will eventually become insufficient and the airplane will start to fall. Learning to recover from a stall is one of the first and most important things included in initial flight training.

High-speed buffet is encountered as the wings approach the speed of sound (Mach 1.0). Any object that moves through the air at a speed below Mach 1.0 produces a "sound" wave out ahead of it that gently begins moving the air out of the way as the object approaches. This facilitates a smooth flow of air around the object. As the speed increases toward Mach 1.0, the object begins to catch up with this "sound" wave in front of it until the point where the air is no longer moving out of the way and—BAM!—the object abruptly "slams" against the wall of air. A shock wave results which can be heard as an audible sonic boom that disrupts the airflow around the object. The resulting turbulent flow around an airplane approaching Mach 1.0 is called high-speed buffet.

The airspeed at which low-speed buffet occurs *increases* with altitude. Conversely, the airspeed at which high-speed buffet occurs *decreases* with altitude. For subsonic aircraft, the two speeds eventually meet. At that point it is impossible for the wings to create enough lift to support the airplane and gravity will begin to take over, causing it to fall. This convergence is so serious that it is referred to as "coffin corner." Airline crews typically maintain a wide margin away from these limits. The published altitude limitation for the B-757 is 42,000 feet, but even this is only possible if the air temperature and aircraft weight are low enough to get that high.

That night we were enroute to Miami, Florida (MIA). A long

line of thunderstorms had developed between Texas and North Carolina. We were trying to pick our way through the gaps, but the holes started closing up. We didn't have enough fuel to go around the line, so we decided to go over the storms. We climbed up to 41,000 feet, which gave us a few thousand feet of clearance above the storms, so we started to cross over the top. Unfortunately, those pesky storms kept growing higher and higher. Before long, we were getting bumped around in the tops of the clouds. The decision to cross over the top was proving to be unwise and we had painted ourselves into a corner. Turning around would have only made things worse, so we continued.

The only option we had left was to climb, so we slowly inched our way up to 42,000 feet. This put us unnervingly close to the airplane's coffin corner. The margin between high- and low-speed buffet was less than 15 knots (1 knot = 1.15 mph) and the airspeed was bouncing around wildly. We bumped along in this condition for the next several minutes, sweating bullets the whole time. This was a really bad idea, but the only way out was to continue to the other side. I have to say this was the most nerve-racking experiences I've ever faced in an airplane. The threat of hitting either limit was weighing ominously on our minds and adrenaline had us on edge. The result would have been a tumble down into the teeth of the storm below us, which could have been catastrophic.

After several torturous minutes we finally emerged on the eastern side of the storm front. What a relief! I took some deep breaths and thought to myself, "*I'm never doing that again.*"

Captain's Log, Airdate 120628

Short Cut

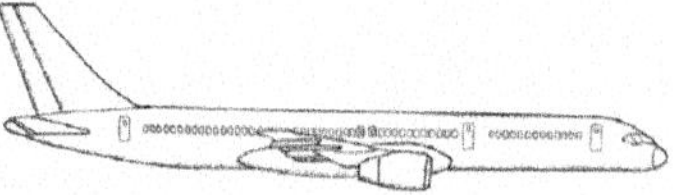

Aircraft: B-757
Crew: Captain Jeff

We were on our way to New York, New York (JFK) flying over the Great Lakes Region and apparently we weren't going fast enough. There was a 747 behind us that was also bound for JFK that was closing the distance between us. Air Traffic Control (ATC) asked the 747 crew to slow down. They acknowledged the request but continued to creep closer. This exchange repeated two more times, but they clearly weren't complying, which was a bit irritating. Then the controller asked if we could take a vector (off-course heading) for spacing. We replied, "Affirmative." This is not unusual in busy airspace. ATC gives someone a brief turn for a few minutes to create more spacing between airplanes that are on the same route. This, however, was not a normal vector. He asked us to turn 90 degrees off course. Now I was really irritated, as it became clear that the purpose for the vector was to accommodate the 747 behind us who was not complying with the controller's instructions.

Despite the nuisance, we had agreed to the vector, so we didn't complain. We turned off course and the 747 pulled ahead of us. We would now be following him the rest of the way to JFK.

The typical arrival sequence for us on that route was to cross over the top of LaGuardia Airport (LGA) at 17,000 feet, then turn south and descend out over the ocean. As soon as we were low enough to make a normal approach, the controller would give us a turn back to the north and clear us for the approach. With this in mind, the strategy after crossing LGA was to descend as quickly as possible to avoid an extended southbound heading away from the airport. This is exactly what I did and our descent quickly outpaced the 747 in front of us. He apparently was not familiar with this strategy. The result was that the controller gave us the turn back to the airport in front of the 747 which was still well above us.

We had almost reached our gate by the time the 747 touched down. Karma!

Captain's Log, Airdate 120000

Eyes Glued on the Captain

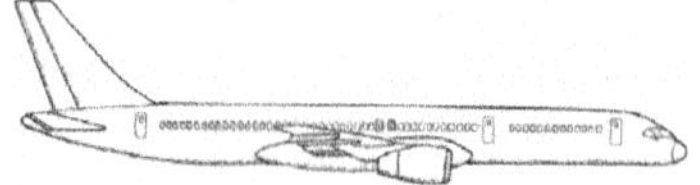

Aircraft: B-757

I learned a lot of important lessons at National Airlines. The following story represents one of those lessons that I would like to highlight. While I was not involved in any of the following incidents, I got the information from my friend in the safety department who had participated in the investigation.

On three separate occasions, airplanes were taxied into contact with the jetway while being directed by the marshaller. This is something that should never happen. The crew places a certain level of trust in the ground crew because it is impossible for them to see all that can be seen from the ground position. This is the reason for having ground personnel provide guidance in tight spaces. After the third incident, a comprehensive investigation was conducted.

The smoking gun was finally discovered in a training manual. The instructions directed the marshaller to maintain eye contact with the captain at all times. The purpose of this directive was to ensure that the marshaller maintained an awareness of his position relative to the captain. Because the 757 sits so high off the ground, it can be easy to get caught under the nose, blocking the line of sight with the captain. Unfortunately, some personnel had interpreted that phrase to mean that the marshaller had to keep his eyes glued on the captain. In all three cases, the wing walkers (the ones positioned near the wing) were yelling and waving their arms to signal a stop, but they remained unseen because of the marshaller's tunnel vision on the captain.

> **DEFINITION**
>
> Marshaller:
> The guy on the ground with the wands that uses a system of hand signals to direct the crew in the tight spaces around the gates.

Two important lessons: First, the crew should always be careful about blindly trusting the marshaller. If something doesn't look right, stop and verify. Second, make sure manuals are understood in the larger context of the objective. This is critically important for anyone learning from a manual. Understanding the objective allows us to recognize erroneous interpretations. If the manual phrasing doesn't ensure the objective, either there is some kind of misunderstanding involved or the manual needs to be changed (or both).

Unemployment

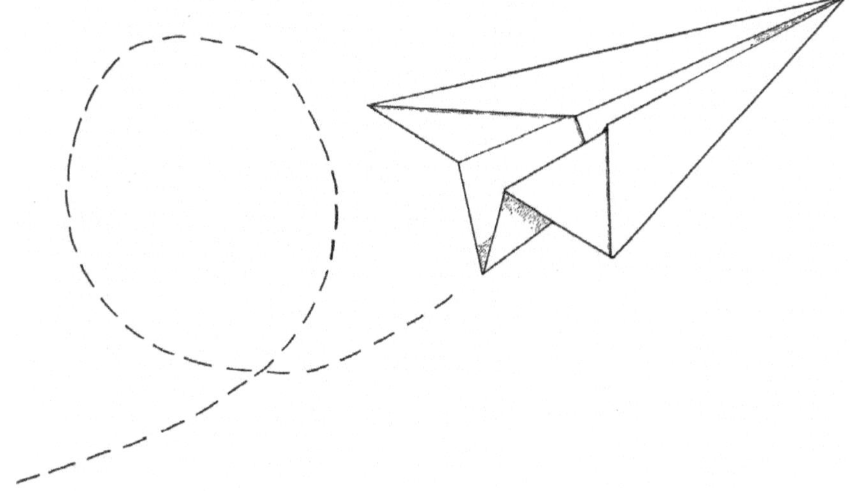

The final demise of National Airlines came somewhat suddenly and I found myself unemployed for the first time in my airline career. Even though National was a great experience for me, there was something wrong. I wasn't happy and I couldn't wrap my mind around what the problem was. Maybe I was simply burned out and I needed a break. I was looking all over the world for an airline job, but I couldn't get any response. I had been working part-time as a representative for a brokerage firm, so I transitioned to doing that full time.

The most important lesson I learned during that time was how much I loved flying. I missed it! I missed the satisfaction of taming big jets. I missed the sights and sounds. I missed the flight deck camaraderie. I missed the jump-seat privileges (the ability to get on any airline any time and go anywhere for free).

I was unemployed for six months, which is a long time in the airline industry. Pilot skills are perishable and it gets increasingly difficult to find a job as those skills deteriorate. A few weeks after National died, a captain with whom I had flown several times asked me to help him reposition one of the stranded airplanes at the request of the leasing company. During that flight, we discussed what lay ahead for each of us and he asked me to send him a résumé. He didn't have any specific plans, but he wanted it in case he came across an opportunity for me. I gave him a copy. Nothing happened for several weeks and I forgot about it.

Just as hope was beginning to fade, I got an unexpected call from a small airline. I had only heard of this company once before, but they had plans for expansion and their chief pilot had received that résumé from my friend. A few days later I found myself sitting in a training class at their headquarters.

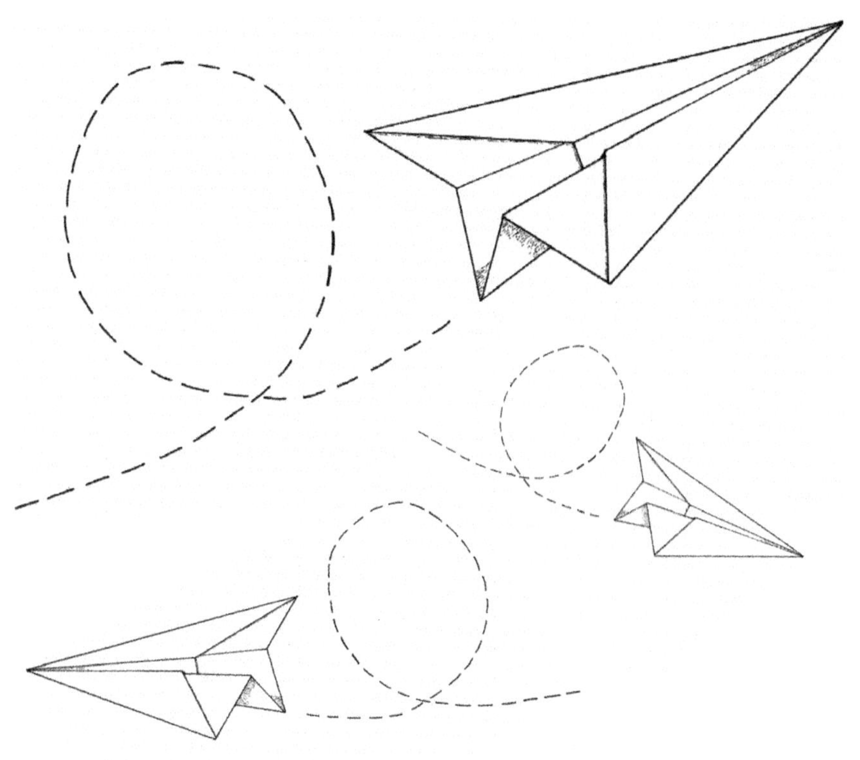

Career Airline

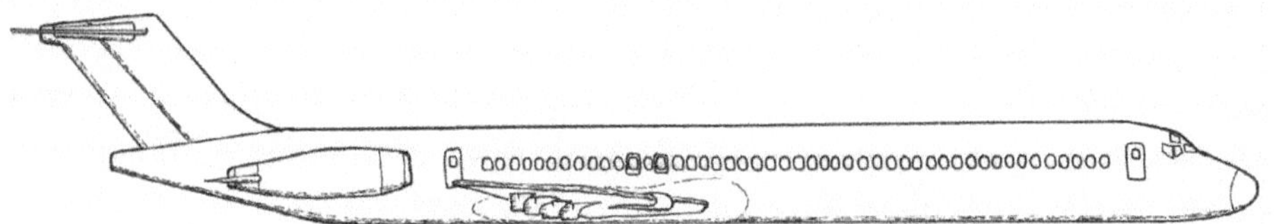

I began working at an upstart airline that was a fascinating little enterprise when I came on the scene. It was an insignificant speck in the industry, with only four airplanes, two of which were being used exclusively for charter operations. It had just emerged from bankruptcy with an infusion of funding and expertise, but there were a lot more questions than answers at that point. While most pilots at the time were passing on it as too risky, it was a unique opportunity for me and my family.

The new management team was planning to build a fleet of McDonnell-Douglas MD-80s at a time when other airlines were getting rid of them in favor of newer, more efficient aircraft. This lack of efficiency meant they were almost being given away. These old workhorses were being acquired for the price of two engines; the airplane was basically free. The bargain price was something the company was planning to exploit.

Affectionately (or derisively) known as the "Mad Dog", this loud, gas-guzzling airliner was coming to the end of its run in the industry. While it lacked the latest bells and whistles, the Mad Dog was still a sturdy workhorse with a lot of life left in it. It's built like a tank. Douglas Aircraft had originally designed and built this jet in the 1960s with the designation DC-9. As the airline world moved into the computer age in the 1980s, it was given a digital facelift and additional length to the cabin. The newly merged McDonnell-Douglas company decided to change the new designation to MD-80. American Airlines acquired a very large fleet of them, which they designated as the "Super 80" for marketing purposes. She has earned a reputation now for many years among the pilots who have flown her as a quirky but reliable workhorse.

One of the most glaring weaknesses of the Mad Dog is runway performance. While most modern jets have ultra-efficient wings and high-bypass (more thrust at slower speeds) jet engines, the MD-80 is still stuck, aerodynamically speaking, in a virtual 1960s time warp. The bottom line is that it needs longer runways to lift itself off the ground. Our company further compounded this performance challenge by filling the cabin with as many revenue passengers as possible and flying long stage lengths (airline term for flight distance). While the fuel tanks had the capacity to hold enough fuel for 2,000-mile flights and longer, it was always a challenge to lift that much weight off the ground on takeoff.

My biggest challenge in adapting to the MD-80 was that I had most recently come from the Boeing 757, which is a great airplane in almost every respect. The 757 was one of Boeing's greatest achievements and I loved flying it. A couple years went by before I finally developed a tolerance for the Mad Dog, but eventually I arrived at a point that I would describe as a love-hate relationship. My new-hire pilot class included three friends who had flown 757s for the recently-shuttered National Airlines. Matt, one of those friends, summed it up like this: "You know what our problem is? Now that we've flown the 757, we're ruined for life." I couldn't disagree with him. The bar had been set so high and it would affect our perceptions for the rest of our careers.

Ultimately, I'm grateful I had the opportunity to fly the MD-80 for so long. It provided a learning opportunity for me to develop a high level of mastery over a big jet. I reached a point of supreme confidence. I could make it do anything and I was always way ahead of it. My experience eventually led me to a position to teach all aspects of the airplane in the classroom and the simulator. I had the pleasure of introducing its quirks and capabilities to new-hire first officers and also to sharpen the understanding and skills of new captain trainees. It was a good thirteen years of flying and learning.

Captain's Log, Airdate 140811

Ramp Standoff

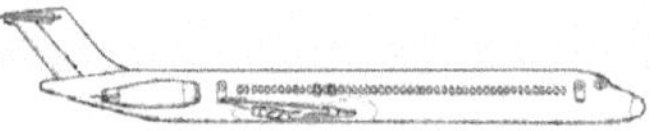

Aircraft: MD-80
Crew: Captain Dave

Our company was growing but we were still a very small carrier, even at our home base. We shared our gates with a major US carrier that I will call Bigtime Airlines. We were the new kids on the block and most of Bigtime's personnel didn't like us encroaching on their territory. They weren't shy about it, either.

Upon arrival at our home base, ramp control instructed us to hold for traffic blocking access to our gate. Our company aircraft was being pushed off that gate to reposition to the overnight parking area and there wasn't enough room to get past them. While waiting, we heard a Bigtime crew report in behind us, facing the same situation. They were instructed to hold *behind us* for the outbound aircraft. It would only be a few minutes and there was no other option, so we all waited and watched. Once the tug disconnected, our maintenance crew was instructed to taxi out of the alleyway. They began, then suddenly stopped. This didn't make sense and now we were confused.

After a few seconds, our maintenance guys asked about the other airplane blocking their way. At this point we noticed that the Bigtime 757 had pulled up along-side us, creating unnecessary congestion and confusion. What should have been routine was now a problem and the following exchange went something like this:

Ramp Control: Newtown maintenance, can you get around the Bigtime 757?
Our Maintenance: I think so.
Ramp Control: Newtown maintenance, taxi around the Bigtime to parking.
Our Maintenance: Roger. Taxi around the Bigtime to parking.
Ramp Control: Bigtime, hold for the Newtown outbound then taxi to the gate.
Bigtime: Roger. Bigtime will hold for the Newtown outbound then to the gate.
Ramp Control: Newtown give way to company outbound and Bigtime inbound, then taxi to the gate.

I was rather irritated that the controller was accommodating the Bigtime crew that disregarded their instructions and created a conflict, so my response was snarky:

Me: Roger. Newtown will give way to company outbound and to the Bigtime who just—can't—seem—to wait.

FUN FACT

Air Traffic Control is divided into several different areas, each with their own function: ramp, ground, tower, approach, etc. Ramp Control directs traffic around the gates.

Silence ensued and nobody moved. After a pause the ramp controller sheepishly verified my response:

Ramp Control: Newtown, verify you're giving way to the Bigtime 757?

Me: Yes, sir. Newtown will give way to the Bigtime who just—can't—seem—to wait.

Again there was silence and nobody moved. After a longer pause, the controller changed his mind:

Ramp Control: Bigtime, hold your position.

Bigtime (with a tone of resignation): Roger. Hold position.

Ramp Control: Newtown, give way to company outbound then taxi to the gate.

This was not my objective nor my expectation, but I was happy to accept the change of heart. We taxied to the gate and our passengers deplaned. As we were finishing up and shutting down the airplane for the night, our mechanic (having parked the other aircraft and hurried back to our gate) came on board asking who had said all that. I confessed it was me and he shook my hand approvingly. I pointed out that my objective was not to change the controller's mind, I was just frustrated at the situation and voiced it. He still considered me the hero for the night.

Captain's Log, Airdate 140901

Prank the Check Airman

Aircraft: MD-80

Crew: Check Airman Marty

FUN FACT

Anytime a pilot begins flying a new airplane and/or upgrades to captain, a period of IOE under the supervision of a specially-qualified check airman is required.

Our new airline was just entering an amazing growth curve. It was unusual to spend more than one year in the right seat. It was an exciting time and fun to be a part of this dynamic growth. I had finished my upgrade training in the MD-80 and it was my first day of required Initial Operating Experience (IOE). Supervising my operations as a new captain was Marty, one of the most senior and highly-respected check airmen in the company. I was looking forward to the opportunity to learn from him.

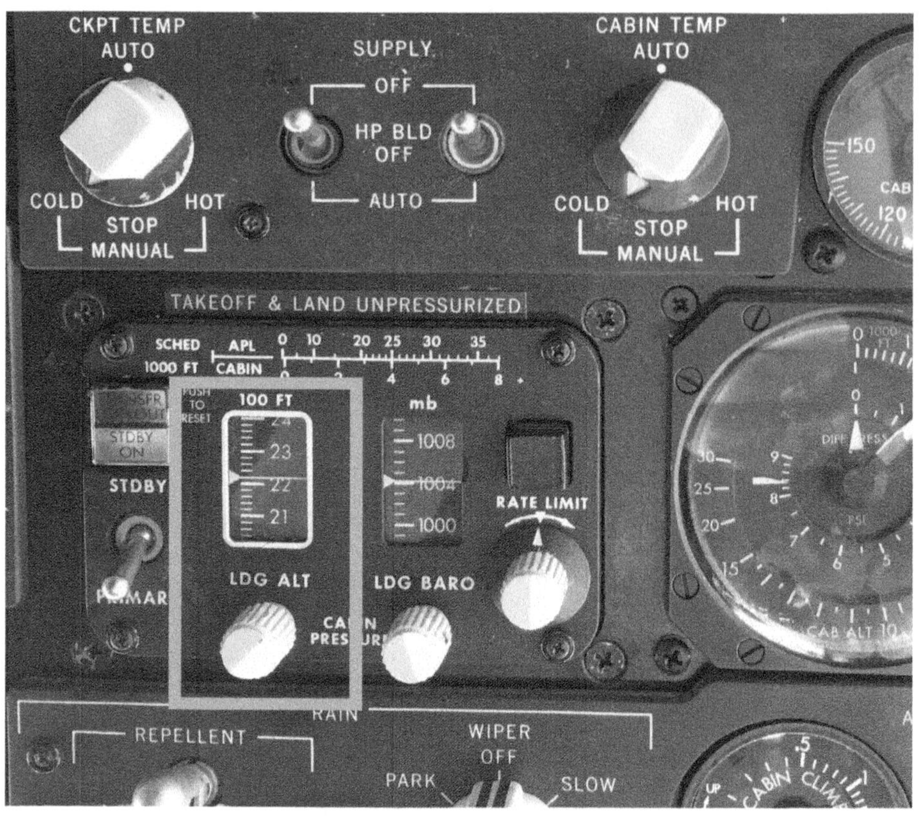

MD-80 Pressurization Panel. The elevation of the landing airport (in the box) needed to be set for each flight.

I had worked my last flight as a first officer (FO) with Captain Dave just a few days earlier. Wanting to mess with Marty, Dave put me up to a little prank. One of the required actions for each flight on an MD-80 is to reset the pressurization system to the landing elevation of the next airport (see illustration). It was an unwritten expectation for the FO to do this as soon as practical after landing. Dave knew that Marty was a big proponent of this simple between-flight action. The planned prank was to watch Marty closely to see if I could catch him failing to do it and then say, "You know, some of the better FOs will go ahead and set the altitude for the next leg."

As luck would have it, Marty missed it on our first leg and I followed through with the plan. He quickly pulled back and glared searchingly at me. I thought I was about to get a tongue-lashing and I was beginning to regret the whole thing. Then, surprisingly, he started backpedaling and offering every justification he could think of for his misstep. I didn't let him go very long before I stopped chuckling and let him in on it.

I have thought about this situation many times since then. It was funny in the moment, but he also reminded me again of an important leadership lesson. He had every right to put me in my place as a sassy new captain who didn't know much, but he didn't. He recognized his mistake and respected the fact that I was calling him out for it. Instead of playing the experience card, he deferred to me as a qualified crew member.

Captain's Log, Airdate 141011

Did We Miss the Dog?

Aircraft: MD-80
Crew: First Officer Gary
Flight Attendant Cheri

When you develop an expectation in your mind that doesn't turn out that way, it can be helpful as a cross check against what is going on. If anything doesn't look right/sound right/seem right, a flashing light goes off in your mind and nudges you to dig deeper to find out why. Some call this concept TLAR (That Looks About Right); if it doesn't look right then there might be a problem. That expectation, however, can sometimes lead to tunnel vision that blocks out your ability to see the correct way because you're too zeroed in on what you're expecting.

A flight is never over until the engines are shut down and the last checklist is complete. Passengers tend to look at the landing as the end of the flight and we sometimes hear applause after landing. In reality, the segment from landing to the gate can be one of the busiest parts of a flight that is most fraught with threats. It's important to stay focused during this critical phase of flight.

As we taxied to the terminal, Gary confirmed gate six. For whatever reason, I created an expectation in my mind of going to gate four. As we approached the gate, I didn't even notice the ground crew at six because my tunnel vision was focused on four and I wondered why there was nobody waiting for us there. As I continued past six, Gary called it to my attention. I abruptly applied the brakes and made the correction back toward six. It was a rookie mistake and I was glad Gary was paying attention.

Cheri, one of my all-time favorite flight attendants, was the lead. After we reached the gate and opened the door she quickly asked (referencing the sudden stop), "Did we miss the dog?" It was moments like this that made her so endearing.

Captain's Log, Airdate 141030

Slip, Sliding Away

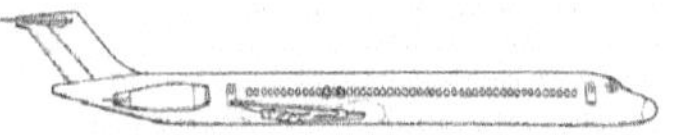

Aircraft: MD-80

Crew: First Officer Garrison

This was a great example of the flight not being over until arriving safely at the gate with the brakes set.

As a new captain at the bottom of the seniority list, schedules tend to get changed around. When something goes wrong with the operation, the brain trust in dispatch starts shuffling the available assets like pieces on a chess board. Unfortunately, pilots are among those pieces. This was a charter that was scheduled to take a film crew from our home base to Detroit, Michigan (DTW) and then return empty back home. While en route to DTW an incident occurred at one of our stations that slightly damaged the aircraft on the ground there. A decision was made (moving pieces) to send us there after DTW to make a swap with the damaged airplane.

We ferried our empty plane there, where the weather had turned a bit ugly. An early-season storm was dumping snow on the area, which presented two important considerations. First, is there enough visibility to see the runway for landing? We usually need at least one-half mile visibility. Second, is it too slick on the runway to stop our 40-ton aircraft from sliding off? This is called "braking action."

Visibility was sufficient to see the runway without any problem and the diligent snow-plow work had left us with good braking action, so the landing was uneventful. As I turned off the runway it was clear that the taxiways had not received the same attention from the snow plows, so I slowed to a cautious crawl as we proceeded to the gate. The entry to the terminal ramp required a 90-degree turn, so I applied the brakes to slow even further for the turn, but there was absolutely no effect. This level of braking action is classified as "NIL." In other words, the tires were just sliding along the pavement with no traction at all. This was the first time in my career that I had experienced it.

Rather than attempt a dubious turn, I simply continued straight on the taxiway, aborting the turn to the ramp. I've joked since then that it was the only occasion that I've done a missed approach to the ramp. It took a few minutes to make our way back around to the same point again. This gave the plowing crew an opportunity to clear that area and the second attempt was successful.

DEFINITION

Missed Approach:
A prescribed, in-flight procedure designed to abort an approach and climb up and away from any surrounding obstacles.

We then switched to the damaged airplane. The entry door had a small nick inflicted by the jetway. It was removed from service out of an abundance of caution so we could fly it to our repair shop. We ferried the empty airplane and, upon arrival at the shop, the technicians laughed at us for ferrying it half way across the country for such a tiny nick.

We laughed with them but that is the nature of airline operations. We maintain such large safety margins that even a small nick gets serious attention.

Captain's Log, Airdate 141114

Traffic on the Runway

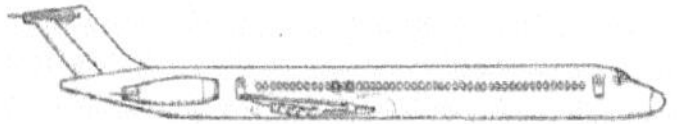

Aircraft: MD-80

Crew: First Officer Mike

Each season has its unique challenges, but winter has the most. The weather today was marginal and dispatch had added an alternate airport with enough fuel to get there after an approach at our destination. Mike was an excellent First Officer. We discussed the situation and still expected to get in without any problems, because the weather wasn't too bad.

Most airports have Instrument Landing Systems (ILS) that provide precise electronic guidance to the runway. This guidance gets us close enough to see the runway and then continue to a landing visually. Even with the precision of the system, it is still important to see the runway. The design is to follow the guidance down to a prescribed minimum altitude. If we can see the runway before we get to that point, we continue to a landing; if not, we execute a "missed approach" that is designed to climb back up and away from the obstacles below. Like most ILS approaches, this one allowed a descent all the way down to 200 feet above the runway before the missed approach was required.

Based on the weather information available, we began the approach with the expectation of seeing the runway at about 500 feet, well before the minimum altitude. As we descended below this point, we were surprised that no signs of the runway were appearing. Then something very unusual happened. At 300 feet, the tower instructed us to "go around" because there was traffic on the runway. I initiated the missed approach, having never seen the runway.

I climbed to a safe altitude, but we were now facing a dilemma. We started the flight with enough fuel to attempt an approach and then continue to our alternate if necessary. Attempting two approaches here was not in the plan. Also, because we had not seen the runway at 300 feet, the success of a second attempt was now questionable. We explained our situation to the approach controller and made a declaration of "minimum fuel," indicating that any further delay would make our fuel situation critical. Now, critical does not mean imminent fuel exhaustion. We always like to have about an hour of fuel in our back pocket, so to speak, and anything less than that is pushing the critical limit. The controller assured us that other aircraft had not had any problems and a second attempt would likely be successful.

These are the critical decisions that rest on a captain's shoulders. There is an obvious expectation to complete the flight as planned, but safety must always trump the lesser considerations. I was fortunate to have Mike's experience and insight available as we discussed our plan. Ultimately, we decided to continue based on the controller's recommendation. If anything went wrong with the second approach, however, we would immediately declare an emergency and proceed to our alternate with priority handling.

It all worked out. We made a second attempt, saw the runway just before the 200-foot minimum altitude and continued to a normal landing from there. Still, we breathed a sigh of relief once the wheels were safely on the ground.

Captain's Log, Airdate 141221

What a Bad Landing!

Aircraft: MD-80
Crew: First Officer Joel
Flight Attendant Carmen

It was my leg and I made a genuinely bad landing. Passengers and flight attendants like to make judgements about landings and then make comments to the flight crew, but there is no way to judge a landing from the cabin. I know what a good landing is and there is no way I can make an assessment about it without seeing it from the flight deck. Those in the cabin make their judgements based on the smoothness of the touchdown. While a soft touchdown might feel good, it might also be a terrible landing. The most important aspect is to land in the right spot (on the centerline and not too far down the runway). We all love a smooth-as-silk landing, but it's not okay for a pilot to give up too much runway to get it. It happens too often.

I've thought about this dilemma too many times to count,

considering possible solutions. I think the best way is for pilots to hold each other accountable, so I created a point system to objectively rate landings based on the following criteria (from highest importance to lowest):

1. In the touchdown zone (3 points)
2. On the runway centerline (3 points)
3. At the correct speed (2 points)
4. Aligned with the runway (1 point)
5. Touching down smoothly (1 point)

As indicated, a smooth touchdown is the least important factor. Based on my own point system, this landing was a five at best. I've made some bad landings in my career, but this was one of the worst. We hit the runway with a vengeance. Fortunately, MD-80s are built like tanks. Joel laughed at me most of the way to the gate. Then it got worse after the passengers had deplaned. Carmen hobbled past me holding her back, moaning in mock pain. I had no choice but to laugh at myself. Win some, lose some.

DEFINITION

Touchdown Zone: The beginning part of the runway length from 1,000 feet to 3,000 feet. It is indicated by painted markings on the runway.

Captain's Log, Airdate 141224

The Private Family Jet

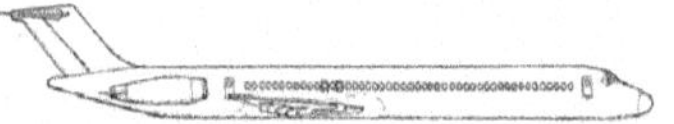

Aircraft: MD-80

Crew: First Officer Joel

It was Christmas Eve and I was the junior captain assigned to the worst trip of the month: ferrying an empty aircraft to one of our other bases on Christmas Eve for it to be used on a charter to the Caribbean and back on Christmas Day. The charter would be flown by a crew from the other base, while we would wait for their return. This meant sitting in a hotel until late on Christmas Day before we could ferry the airplane back home. The situation was especially sad because I had five young children at the time.

I was given a lemon and I decided to make lemonade. I got permission to take my family with me and the CEO himself approved an extra hotel room for us to have Christmas Day together. It was a once-in-a-lifetime opportunity to take my family on a private jet for a Christmas vacation. Because the flight was not open to the public, I was able to leave the flight deck door open to allow my family to see what Dad does at work. Because my children had mostly always known Christmas in the desert, it was an added bonus for them to have some "winter wonderland" fun in the snow. It was a magical holiday adventure and a treasured memory for all of us.

Captain's Log, Airdate 141226

Emergency Descent!

Aircraft: MD-80
Crew: First Officer Joel

I've made plenty of mistakes as a captain—some worse than others. This was toward the bad end of the scale. It was wintertime and keeping the cabin warm was a priority, but the temperature controls on the MD-80 can be temperamental. There's an art form to getting the temperature right in that airplane. The design is a lot like a typical home thermostat in that you set the desired temperature and let it work automatically. Unfortunately, that didn't always work. Today was one of those days. We tried to coax the system to work automatically, but it wasn't responding.

Plan B involves using manual controls to force the system to respond. The trade-off is that the automatic overheat protection is lost. The system will give you exactly what you ask for right up until it overheats and automatically shuts down. It is important to note that the system that maintains the temperature is integrally linked to the pressurization of the cabin. If the system overheats, the source of pressurization (called a "pack") goes with it. Given the obvious importance of pressurization, there are two packs to ensure redundancy. With this in mind, the crew should avoid putting both controllers in manual at the same time. I don't remember ever being taught this important point in any of my training, but the Mad Dog was about to teach me herself.

One of the system packs did overheat and shut down. Presented with this failure, we began working the problem. We followed the checklist procedures and then I made a radio call to our company to apprise them of the situation. The frequency was busy, so I had to wait a few minutes. Unfortunately, the very moment my maintenance guy answered the radio call, the second pack shut down as well. Uh oh! We now had no sources of pressurization. I stared at the panel in disbelief for a moment. We were about to lose pressurization at 33,000 feet.

"We need to go down, down, down. Now, now, now!" was my excited response. We donned our oxygen masks. Joel got a descent clearance and smoothly initiated an emergency descent. Fortunately, two things worked in our favor: first, the pressure seals on this plane were fairly tight and, second, it didn't take long for our packs to cool down and come back on line. Thus, we did not reach the threshold for automatic deployment of the cabin oxygen masks before normal operation was restored. With no additional issues, we continued to our destination with nothing more than bruised egos. When I asked the flight attendants later about the emergency

FUN FACT

Environmental control on a jet aircraft is provided by pressurization "packs." These packs use pressurized air that is bled off the engine to heat or cool the air and then pump it into the cabin to maintain a comfortable temperature and pressure.

descent, they asked, "What emergency descent?" Joel had done the whole thing so smoothly that nobody noticed, yet so quickly that the masks didn't deploy.

I learned a valuable lesson that night without too much pain and anguish. I never again put both controllers in manual at the same time and I made sure to emphasize the point years later when training new pilots in the MD-80.

Captain's Log, Airdate 150219

Steering Problems

Aircraft: MD-80
Crew: First Officer Del
Relief Captain Bill

Another day, another costly mistake. Today's mission was a charter flight to the Caribbean. The route would take us to Punta Cana, Dominican Republic, which would stretch the capability of the MD-80 to its limit with a full load of travelers and their baggage and enough fuel to make it that far. We used every strategy we could to save weight and ended up without a single pound to spare, a takeoff weight of 160,000 pounds. Additionally, the distribution of the load was to the forward balance limit for the aircraft.

It was scheduled to be a very long day, so our crew included a relief captain, Bill. We would each take turns flying to ensure none of us would exceed our flight time limitations for the day. All three of us had been at our respective positions for less than six months.

Large airplanes are equipped with a provision that disables the hydraulic steering while being pushed back from the gate. Without this safety measure, it's possible that the hydraulic steering control could flip the tug over when it is attached to the nose gear. After pushback, the ground crew easily returns the steering to normal by disengaging this bypass feature. The MD-80 has a weakness in this system that occasionally prevents the steering bypass from unlatching after pushback.

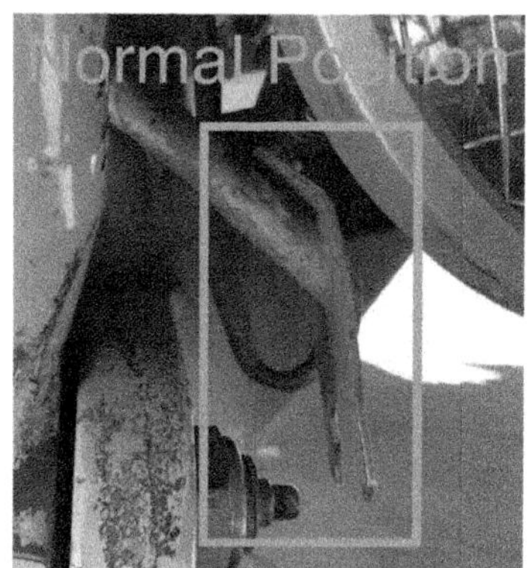

These two photos show the steering bypass lever in the normal and the bypass positions.

We loaded up and pushed back, but I found the steering was locked when I began to taxi. We reasoned together that the steering bypass problem could not be the issue we were facing because the steering was not bypassed but, instead, was stuck. I taxied a few feet and nothing changed. I did it again and the steering tiller abruptly lurched to the left. We were now stuck in place. We called the ground crew back out and they reported to us that the nose tires were flat. We consulted together again and decided this must be the reason why the steering was stuck. With no way to move, we shut down the engines and I got out to inspect the nose tires. I discovered the left tire was flat. It all made sense to me at that point.

We arranged for buses to come out to the aircraft to unload our passengers and return them to the terminal. This is where the story took a strange turn. As the people deplaned, reducing the weight, the nose gear eventually straightened itself out and, *voila*, the tire was no longer flat. I was completely stunned!

After several minutes, a contract mechanic showed up. I had never met this guy before and he was telling me that there was nothing wrong with the nose gear. I knew what I had seen and could not reconcile with the idea that nothing was wrong. We were unable to come to a resolution, so dispatch sent another airplane from our home base with two new nose tires and a trusted company mechanic to fix the airplane, causing an eight-hour delay. Obviously, *nobody* was happy!

When we finally got underway again, everybody was somewhat beleaguered, but the second attempt went just fine. It's a long flight to Punta Cana and along the way we discussed at length what had happened. We came to the idea that perhaps the incident was indeed what we had learned in training about the steering bypass not unlatching. We also decided we could prove our theory. After landing, Bill went down to the nose wheel and held the bypass latch in place while I attempted to move the steering. It was locked just the same as it had been before.

The whole sequence of events now came clearly into focus. The bypass did not properly disengage after pushback. The result was a steering tiller that was locked in place. With the extreme weight distribution on the nose wheels the tire got smashed flat when the steering lurched that direction. Then, as the people deplaned and the weight reduction released the tension, it straightened out and the tire returned to form with no indication of having been flat. At this point we all felt rather frustrated that we had misunderstood what was presented to us in training. The whole fiasco could have easily been avoided.

Adding to the misery, the rescue flight had left the "chess board" in dispatch with one less airplane in our home base, so they asked us if we were able to return all the way back. I told Del and Bill that I knew I would be too tired for such a long flight. They said they were okay, so we agreed to the extended day. We flew our empty plane to Orlando, Florida in order to clear United States Customs and then continued to our home base, arriving the following morning. It had been a total of 26 long hours on duty for us that day.

A few days later I found myself talking with our Director of Flight Operations. I apologized to him and took responsibility for the incident, but I also pointed out how the misunderstood training had led all three of us to the same erroneous conclusion. We had cost the company a lot of money that day and caused a major disruption to the operation. He could have taken a very harsh position and I was the captain responsible for the whole thing. His response was pure gold for me:

He asked, "Did you call maintenance?"

My response, "Yes."

"Did you do what they told you to do?"

Again, "Yes."

"So what else were you supposed to do?"

"True, but I felt bad that I caused such a problem."

His priceless response: "Don't worry about it."

Again I learned a lesson without suffering terribly harsh consequences. Of course, I never let that happen again and, when I later became an instructor, I made sure that new pilots understood what happened when the steering bypass failed to unlatch.

Captain's Log, Airdate 150407

Fuel Lever Scare

Aircraft: MD-80

Crew: First Officer Del

Levers and switches are not typically out of position and those that serve a vital function are checked as part of a prescribed procedure. Checklists are extremely valuable to ensure everything is set where it should be, but even the best checklist can sometimes miss something. Fuel levers (see illustration) are critical items that must be in the correct position. They control the fuel valves going to the engines, either off or on. Our procedure covered the fuel levers as part of the preflight preparation and I ensured they were off. After I had done this, the flight attendants informed me that the Public Address (PA) system in the cabin was set too low. I called maintenance to come take care of the issue and then resumed my preparations for the flight.

When the mechanic arrived, he turned on the right fuel lever as part of the process to trouble shoot the PA system. There's a micro switch built into the lever that senses its position for use in various functions. In this case it was the input used for the PA system to determine ground mode versus flight mode. The PA volume is automatically stepped up while in flight mode (engines running). The mechanic placed the fuel lever in the *on* position to do his check, but then he forgot to return it back *off* after he was done. He correctly adjusted the PA, but left me in a difficult spot because of his oversight. I was not aware that the lever had been moved.

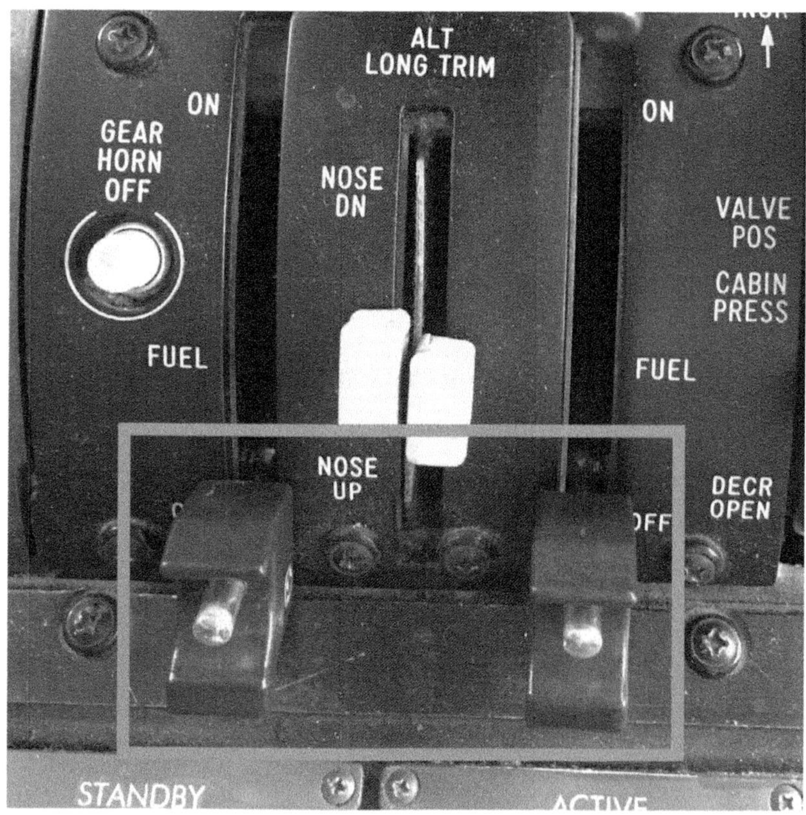

The two engine fuel control levers (in the box) are shown in the off position.

Jet engines are amazing machines. They use spinning blades to suck air into the front end and compress it in the middle where fuel is added and ignited to force a powerful jet of airflow out the back. The way we start these powerful engines is by "blowing" an external pressurized air source into the engine much like a pinwheel to get it spinning up to a minimum speed. The minimum rotation is necessary to ensure sufficient airflow through the engine before adding and lighting the fuel. The "fire" burning inside a running engine is extremely hot, but the airflow ensures that the majority of that heat is directed out the back so as not to burn up anything in the middle. Starting engines is a simple, routine process that is repeated at the beginning of each flight.

I began starting the right engine as I had done so many times before. I opened the start valve and watched the engine spin up to the minimum RPM. I then reached for the fuel lever to switch it on, but was horrified to realize it was already there. Adrenaline shot through my body as I quickly moved my eyes to the temperature indication. As a relatively new captain, I was terrified that I had just burned up a two-million-dollar engine. To my surprise, the temperature had not yet exceeded the limit and I quickly turned the fuel back off again while continuing to spin the engine to keep the cooling airflow moving through it.

Once the engine was secure, I took a deep breath. I was obviously grateful that the engine was not damaged, but I was angry that the mechanic had left the fuel lever on. I was also frustrated that I hadn't caught it myself before the start sequence. It was a cascade of emotion as I came back down from my adrenaline rush. I made a determination after that to add my own extra step to ensure the fuel levers were off *immediately before* engine start.

Captain's Log, Airdate 150706

Fake Wind

Aircraft: MD-80

Crew: First Officer Denny

We were on the last leg of a long charter trip. I was in the left seat for what looked to be a beautiful, trouble-free flight home. As we reached our cruise altitude, Air Traffic Control (ATC) gave us a slight shortcut direct to Kansas City. I entered it into the Flight Management System (FMS) to reset our course. This is something we do every day. Almost all modern navigation is done with some type of FMS and it's wonderfully useful when it works.

A lot of people have the idea that pilots turn on the autopilot and then don't do anything for hours, but this is not true. Even though the computer is guiding the airplane, I always keep an eye on it to make sure it's doing what it's programmed to do. I'm always listening to and feeling the airplane, even smelling for anything unusual. As I kept an eye on our progress, I noticed the heading was creeping northward. This is not unusual because the FMS automatically corrects for wind in order to maintain the programmed course. As the heading continued to creep north, however, the computed wind data was becoming less believable. I compared it to the forecast data we were given as part of our flight plan and it wasn't making sense. Eventually it was indicating more than a 200-knot crosswind and the airplane was correcting into this "wind."

I pointed it out to Denny. We could tell something was wrong, but we couldn't put a finger on what the problem was or how to fix it. We were in the middle of this process of trying to figure it out when ATC finally intervened, asking us to verify we were proceeding direct to Kansas City.

"Uh, yes sir. We're direct Kansas City."

"Well I'm showing you tracking fifteen degrees north of course."

Clearly something was off, so we gave up on the FMS and used the old-school, radio navigation to fly directly to Kansas City. This particular airplane was not equipped with GPS and the gyroscopic navigational instruments were not as accurate. Sometimes they would drift a bit too far off, but I had never seen such an egregious error. The position calculated by the system was drifting and the computer was simply making up a fake "wind" to account for it. By correcting towards the fictitious north wind, it was tracking well north of course. We decided to reset the position in the FMS to see if we could rein it back in. This immediately fixed the problem and it did not recur the rest of the flight.

It was only a minor hiccup, but I had never seen the FMS do something like that and, in 13 years of flying the MD-80, I never saw it happen again. Sometimes computers just do strange things.

Captain's Log, Airdate 150708

Attendant in the Lavatory

Aircraft: MD-80

Crew: First Officer Mike

Flight Attendant Abbey

Today we encountered one of the strangest issues I've seen. Abbey got stuck in the lavatory. When she tried to come out, the latch would not open. This happened just as we were beginning our descent. We now faced an interesting dilemma: either find a way to get her out, or we would be forced to land that way. I decided to give it a try, but there is always a risk any time we exit the flight deck to the cabin in flight. Could it be a ploy by someone with ill intent to lure us into an ambush in the cabin? We assessed the situation, discussed the risk and determined it was acceptable in this situation. Abbey really was stuck. She was getting anxious and it wasn't a good option to land with her unsecured like that. Also, Mike was one of the best first officers a captain can have. I had no reservations about leaving him solo for a couple minutes.

I went out to the cabin to investigate and left Mike to continue the descent, but the clock was ticking and Abbey was starting to bang on the door. I could see the latch through the small gap, but I needed a screwdriver to slide it open. Of course, no one on the airplane, including the crew, is allowed to carry such a dangerous tool. The best implement I could find was a quarter. Growing up on a farm had taught me the value of resourcefulness and it came in handy that day. It worked! Abbey was elated! And I was a hero for a few minutes.

Captain's Log, Airdate 150922

Hidden Runway

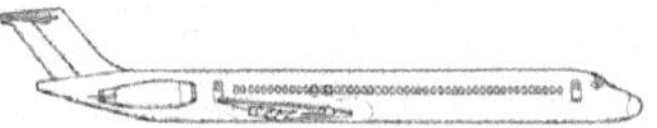

Aircraft: MD-80

Crew: First Officer Kirk

Certain airports are configured for dual use—civilian on one side and military on the other. The destination tonight was one of these. It was a beautiful, clear summer night—a prime opportunity to get lulled into making a mistake.

The two parallel runways 14L (left) and 14R (right) were in use and we could clearly see the airport from over thirty miles out. Approach control cleared us for a visual approach to Runway 14L (civilian side) and handed us off to the tower controller. We checked onto the new frequency and he cleared us to land. This runway is equipped with an Instrument Landing System (ILS) that provides electronic guidance to the runway. We had it set up on our flight guidance panel even though it wasn't needed on such a clear night. This is an important habit that I always keep. Not only is it very useful for vertical guidance while descending to the runway on a dark night, but you never know when it will give you even more helpful information. Tonight it did!

The approach got interesting when I turned to line up with the runway. Kirk noticed it first. The localizer (the lateral guidance portion of the ILS) didn't line up with the runway. We checked our instruments to make sure we hadn't set something wrong, then queried the tower controller to see if the ILS was working correctly. He responded affirmatively. We began scratching our heads, wondering what the problem could be. Just a few seconds later, the lights on 14L came on and we realized we were actually lined up for Runway 14R (the only runway that initially had its lights turned on).

This, of course, was very frustrating. The controller was essentially leading us into a trap. If we hadn't been vigilant, we would have landed on the wrong runway—the military side of the airport. This would have been embarrassing at the very least and even worse if there had been a conflict and they wanted to hang all the blame on us. What saved us was the fact that we had set up the ILS and were paying attention to it even though it was "only" a visual approach. The moral of the story is to never allow yourself to get lulled into complacency and always take advantage of whatever tools are available.

Captain's Log, Airdate 151000

Happy Trails

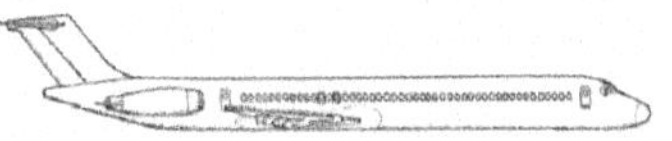

Aircraft: MD-80

Crew: First Officer Curtis

At this point in my career a pleasant little tradition had emerged in the airspace controlled by Denver Center. A veteran controller with a distinctive voice and friendly demeanor had taken up a habit. When he would hand pilots off to the next controller he would always say in a slow drawl, "Have a dandy day." It was something I looked forward to when transitioning through Denver's airspace. This tradition made his retirement a bit sad. A verbal icon was gone.

FUN FACT

The airspace around the world is divided into workable sectors, each headquartered in a major city within its boundaries. Each sector is designated as an enroute control "center" named for that city (e.g. Denver Center).

While thinking about the distinctive tradition during the months after his retirement, I decided to try starting a tradition of my own. I was flying that month with Curtis. One day we had a discussion about what phrase we could use: "Later gator," "Hasta la vista," etc. We shot down a few before we settled on "Happy trails." It was an experiment to see where it would go if we started using it whenever we got handed off. The general response was friendly. It even reached a point that a controller recognized my voice one day and gave me a preemptive "Happy trails" as he handed us off. It was an interesting experiment in the otherwise mundane environment of ATC communications, but I eventually got bored with it after several months and dropped the habit.

Captain's Log, Airdate 151208

Is This One of Our Aircraft?

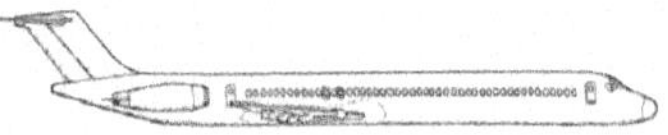

Aircraft: MD-80

Crew: First Officer Mike

One of the byproducts of our growth was constant turnover in the right seat. I flew with new first officers on a regular basis. My first flight with Mike started with a rather memorable moment. He was very smart and skilled but came to us with a significant lack of experience. While he excelled in training, much of what he saw on line was new for him.

Another byproduct of growth was a lot of new aircraft from a diverse list of sources. Our fleet acquisition team was scouring the globe in search of good MD-80s. The majority of our aircraft came from one particular European carrier, so these became our "standard" airplane, but there were significant variations within the fleet. Familiarization with the differences was almost a daily ritual. One of the variants farthest from the norm was aircraft 873. This airplane came from a smaller country with older instrumentation installed. It also had different Flight Management System (FMS) computers with the associated variation in displays. It was an oddball we nicknamed "Woody" due to some non-FAA-approved wooden floorboards in the cargo compartments that had to be changed out before it could be inducted into our fleet.

I was assigned to 873 that day and Mike was on call, like most new pilots. He got a late call out, so I did most of the preparation before he got there. He was in quite a hurry as he stepped into the flight deck that morning. He quickly removed his coat and took a look at the instrument panel. He stopped abruptly. With big eyes and a stressed expression, he asked in disbelief, "Is this one of *our* aircraft?" I smiled and assured him it was, indeed, one of ours. I also reassured him that everything worked mostly the same despite the different appearance.

Captain's Log, Airdate 151200

Red-E-2 Board

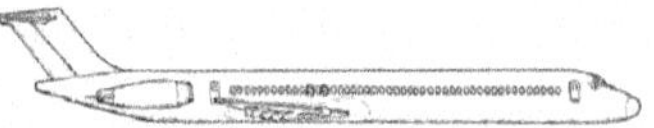

Aircraft: MD-80

My schedule took me to one of my favorite stations so often I was becoming one of the family. I knew everybody there and I looked forward to seeing them week after week.

One of the challenges with operations at that airport is the short runway length. MD-80s and short runways don't go well together. I was always focused on ensuring the best takeoff performance that I could get. The flight from our home base to there was just long enough for the fuel in the wing tanks to get supercooled. Pair this together with the moist coastal air at this station and we would frequently get frost on our wings even with outside temperatures well above freezing. One strategy I often used was to transfer the cold fuel from the wings to the center fuel tank in order to put the warmer fuel from the truck into the wings to melt the frost. It didn't always work, so I always scrutinized the wings very closely to make sure they would be completely clean for maximum performance on takeoff.

Because of my constant scrutiny, the crew there decided to give me a gag gift for Christmas—an ice scraper. It was funny and I appreciated it. My response was to make them a gift of my own. It took a few days for me to make it and I couldn't wait to see their response. I took a small piece of wood, carved the characters E2 into it and painted it red. It was a "red-E-2 board" in reference to the regular back and forth between us about being ready to board or not. They had a good laugh and it became station memorabilia for years thereafter.

Captain's Log, Airdate 160221

Runway Rollercoaster

Aircraft: MD-80

Crew: First Officer Walt

One of the airports we serve has a unique runway. Not only is it short, but the runway slope goes up and down. Going either direction, the runway slopes down for about the first 1500 feet and then back up again. The slope is barely perceptible when just looking at it from the ground, but when an airplane is touching down at 130 knots (150 miles per hour) the anomaly is accentuated. This creates an extra challenge when landing there. If the airplane does not touchdown in the first 1500 feet, the runway starts rising up to smack the landing gear from below.

I liked flying with Walt and it was his turn to land there. It was a good approach, but he floated just long enough for the perfect storm of airplane falling and runway rising. We hit pretty hard! Several items in the cabin were jarred loose. He was rather embarrassed! This unforgiving runway had cut another notch in its belt!

We called a mechanic for an inspection to make sure the airplane was okay to continue. Other than the cabin items that needed to be re-secured, the airframe and landing gear were all good. One of the best characteristics of the MD-80 is its toughness. It's built like a tank; it can take a beating and keep on seating.

Captain's Log, Airdate 160428

Flaps vs. Ailerons

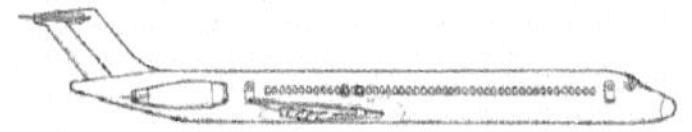

Aircraft: MD-80

Crew: First Officer Jason

Flight Attendant Lonna

Flight Attendant Cheri

Jason has a quick wit with a sarcastic bite. It can be good entertainment on a long day and I always enjoyed flying with him. Today we were flying with a senior cabin crew who may not have been entirely confident in the junior captain.

I always make it a point to listen carefully to reports from flight attendants and passengers, because you don't initially know if their observation might be the sliver of information that could be the key to a successful outcome. Even if their report is *not* useful, it's important to listen anyway to make sure they understand that their input is valued. Again, you never know when it might save the day.

As we taxied out to the runway, we got a call from the cabin indicating that a passenger was concerned that the flaps were split at different angles. A split flap condition can be very dangerous as it would create more lift on one wing than the other, which could potentially roll us upside down on lift off. Of course we took it seriously but our indicator was showing a normal flap position. There are two sets of movable surfaces on the rear edge of the wing: flaps and ailerons. The *flaps* are large and they extend and retract evenly to create more lift for takeoff and landing. The *ailerons* are smaller, are located closer to the wing tips and move *opposite* of each other to intentionally create more lift on one wing in order to roll and turn the aircraft. We decided that the passenger must be looking at the ailerons which were indeed split as they should have been.

This should have been the end of it, but Lonna didn't completely trust the junior captain up front. She called back a couple minutes later to say that the guy was freaking out because of the split flaps. In order to ease their concerns, I sent Jason back to the cabin to visually confirm the position of the flaps. We didn't see any undue risk of him leaving the flight deck since we were on the ground and, if they were right (and the indicators wrong), it would prove to be a vital check. He went back to take a look and returned, confirming that the flaps were indeed normal.

Again, this should have been the end of it, but I think Lonna wanted to make a point so she called again, indicating her opinion that we should return to the gate for a mechanic to look at it because the guy was *really* freaking out. I assured her that nothing was wrong and that we would *not* be returning to the gate. We continued to the runway. It was Jason's leg and, as a part of his takeoff briefing, he asked, "Please, please, can I roll the aircraft just after lift off?" Of course he was being sarcastic, but it still made me laugh.

We took off without any issues and, after we climbed above 10,000 feet, I called the cabin to let them know I would like to have a chat with each of them at some point during the flight to discuss what had happened. When I talked to Cheri, her response was perfect, "Is this going to be the aileron lesson?" Yet another example of why I loved flying with Cheri.

Captain's Log, Airdate 160600

Prophetic Route Map

Aircraft: MD-80

Crew: First Officer Mike

Our procedure on arrival was to pass a note to the station with the arrival information. I started a habit of doodling on these notes during the flight. Whatever was on my mind on a particular day ended up doodled on the arrival note. Today I was thinking about the success we had found at this station and extrapolating where that would lead, so I drew out a potential route map. Mike and I discussed where the logical destinations would be and came up with our best guesses—San Francisco, Los Angeles, Palm Springs, Phoenix, San Diego, etc.

It was just a fun little doodle, but the folks at the station took it as some kind of prophecy. They asked me where I got the information and what I knew. I told them it was nothing more than guess work, but they were inspired by it and pinned it up on the bulletin board in their office. After that day, I would check on it every month or so to see if it was still there. It stayed right there for years. It made me laugh that they took it so seriously. What made it even more funny was to see it gradually unfold much the way I had drawn it up. In the end, I guess it was prophetic.

Captain's Log, Airdate 160811

Birds!

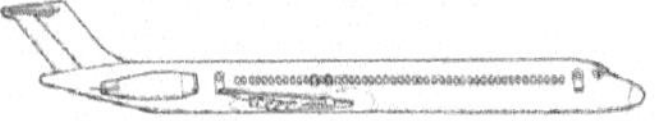

Aircraft: MD-80
Crew: First Officer Jeff
Flight Attendant Diane

Today's trip was to one of our newest and smallest stations. I was flying with Jeff. He had an engineering background and was becoming somewhat of an expert on the MD-80. It was always good to have someone like Jeff as a resource.

It was a beautiful day and it was about to become one of the most memorable of my career. A beautiful day meant birds. Pilots really don't like it when birds hang out near airports. This was years before USAir flight 1549 ended up in the Hudson River, but we all know the dangers. Sadly, bird strikes are not rare. They often result in damage to the aircraft and, obviously, always death to the bird. The USAir 1549 incident involved large fowl, which is less common, but even the small ones we encountered in this case can be hazardous.

It was Jeff's leg and I noticed a flock of small birds on the runway as we accelerated on takeoff. Unfortunately, they didn't move out of our way. I saw one of them come right at my face and I instinctively ducked as it hit the windshield. Too fast to stop, we continued the takeoff. The adventure began after liftoff. Systems started to fail. I called out each failure as it occurred, but the list was starting to pile up and we weren't able to figure out what was wrong. Surely, it was related to the bird strike, but the pieces weren't fitting together such that we could decide what to do about it.

Two of the independent pitot tubes on the front of the aircraft that are used to measure airspeed. There is one more pitot tube (not shown) on the other side.

As we climbed through about 4,000 feet, Jeff noted, "I think we're going faster than what's indicated." I was trying to figure out the mystery from what I could *see*, but Jeff had his hands on the controls and he could *feel* it. My airspeed indicated 210 knots; his showed 210 knots; the standby indicator was at 300. AHA! Now things were starting to make sense. I switched the air data system to source #2 and, voila, both indicator needles popped up to 300 knots. A portion of that small bird had gone straight down my pitot tube (see illustration) before hitting the windshield. It was a one-in-a-million shot to hit that quarter-inch target, but that tube was plugged.

Here is an excellent example of the safety layers in the airline world. Two layers failed today. First was the plugged pitot tube. Second was something very unusual, a concurrent failure of the backup. That system is designed with triple redundancy sourced from three independent pitot tubes (illustration shows two of these three). Number two (Jeff's side) should have provided a normal indication, but that is not what we saw. The third layer was the independent standby system, which worked exactly the way it was supposed to and gave us the information we needed. Fortunately, the system did work normally once I *manually* switched it to the #2 source.

DEFINITION

Pitot Tube:
A small, metal, open-ended tube mounted on the front of an airplane and open to the airstream. It's part of a system that measures airspeed by sensing the pressure of the air being forced into it (i.e. the pressure increases as the airplane goes faster.

With the airspeed indicating correctly, we returned to the airport and Jeff was able to maneuver for a normal landing. Things got even more interesting after we returned to the gate. The first thing I did after opening the door was inspect my pitot tube. I found exactly what we suspected—bird remains. Now the challenge would be to wait a few hours for a spare airplane to arrive. As our passengers deplaned, someone expressed his doubt to me about the "bird" explanation I had given them in flight as the reason for our return. I showed him what was left of the bird and he decided maybe I knew what I was talking about. It always amazes me when people think we're making up imaginary excuses.

Next up was a young boy who looked lost and confused. He was ten years old and his grandparents had cleverly avoided the process (and fee) for an unaccompanied minor (UM) by lying about his age. He didn't know what to do so we were now on child care duty. It took a couple hours for his grandparents to get word and return to the airport. Diane, one of the most professional flight attendants I've worked with, proceeded to kindly explain to them the importance of following the UM guidelines. Their reply, unbelievably, was to throw their grandson under the bus. They said he actually *was* old enough, but he looked younger and had a habit of lying about his age. I could only shake my head in disbelief—and disgust.

Then came the fuel guy. I don't remember what the issue was, but he was getting really animated about something not being right because of "FFA" rules. I tried reasoning with him, but he got more uptight. I finally had to get right up in his face and raise my voice before he decided he could do it the way we needed it done. My crew was shocked! I guess they didn't think I had it in me to be so confrontational. I'm usually so reserved and easy going, saving assertiveness for when it's truly needed.

Dispatch finally rustled up a spare aircraft that arrived more than five hours after the bird strike. A mechanic came with it in order to clean and inspect the system on our wounded airplane. We boarded our beleaguered passengers onto the spare plane and got underway again—seven hours late. At last, we arrived back home—after 3:00 am. What a day!

Captain's Log, Airdate 160817

Where Are We?

Aircraft: MD-80
Crew: First Officer Tina

We were still expanding to more and more cities across the country and it was difficult to keep up sometimes. One of the operational challenges we encountered was limited memory in the Flight Management System (FMS) computers on our aircraft. These computers store important airport data to improve safety and efficiency and reduce workload. With limited memory, sometimes we were going to airports for which we had no data. This practice was certainly not unsafe; every airline had done it for decades before computers were incorporated into modern aircraft. It did, however, place additional workload on us to manually account for the missing data.

Because today's airport was not included in our FMS database, we had to do something to fool the computer. It always requires a pair of airports (both departure and destination) for each flight in order to complete its calculations. Our strategy was to pick the nearest airport that *was* included in the database and use it as a "placeholder" for the departure airport just to satisfy the computer. After takeoff, the airport data was no longer relevant, so we would just navigate from our actual departure point as if we had overflown it.

This practice worked well with one simple caveat: do *not* do a runway update before takeoff. An update was usually accomplished with a single keystroke while in position at the end of the runway in order to ensure the navigational position would be as accurate as possible. The position reset was almost always no more than a slight change to update the computer from its currently calculated position to the known position of the runway from the database. An update was not possible in this case due to the lack of airport data; whatever slight computer errors existed would just be ignored as negligible.

As we reached the end of the runway, Tina went through her normal flow of buttons and switches. Without thinking, she selected runway update and that was it; the FMS now thought it was sitting at the end of the runway at the other airport. At this point we had two options: 1) ignore the computer, takeoff and navigate the old-fashion way using radio signals (more work, more opportunity for errors), or 2) we could take the time to fix it before takeoff. We chose the latter. After several minutes of coaxing we were able to convince the FMS that it was, indeed, at our actual location in order to avoid the extra work enroute.

Captain's Log, Airdate 160828

Let's Back Up

Aircraft: MD-80

Crew: First Officer Brian

The main runway at this small airport had been shortened due to construction during the summer months. The shorter length and the higher temperatures created a performance challenge for the MD-80. Several flights that summer had been forced to include an unscheduled fuel stop because it simply wasn't possible to lift that much fuel, along with a full payload, off that runway. The daily struggle was to find a way to make it work for a nonstop flight.

Today the dispatcher and I had figured out a solution, but it required every last foot of available runway. Most of the time we give up a few feet of runway while turning into position for takeoff. In order to give myself the widest safety margin in this case, I wanted to minimize this loss by making a very tight turn to the centerline. I taxied on to the runway as close as possible to the end and then swung the steering sharply to the left to line up for takeoff.

About half way through the turn the nose-gear steering suddenly lurched farther to the left and got stuck there. At the completion of the turn we were lined up with the runway, but the nose wheel was pointed 90° to the left. I had never heard of this happening before, but now we were stuck and blocking the airport's main runway. We told the tower we would need a minute and I began solving the puzzle.

It occurred to me that the nose gear was probably being held in the perpendicular position by the slight forward-leaning tension created by the engines pushing forward at idle power. I reasoned that if I backed up a few inches it should release. The MD-80 will back up under its own power but this capability is not normally used. Today it was the best solution I could devise. I carefully eased the engines into reverse. I don't know if we actually went backwards or if the tension released before we moved that direction, but the nose wheel slipped right back to its normal position. We were really glad that this ingenious solution had worked. I wasn't sure if I had done something wrong, but everything was normal, so we took off. Despite being proud of my solution, I didn't tell anybody what we had done for fear of criticism.

Years later I found myself in a conversation with the chief pilot and the director of flight operations (my two superiors) and I decided to admit what I had done. Surely the statute of limitations had run out. They listened to my story and the chief pilot then said, "If I had known back then what you had done, I would have given you a commendation for it." I had always felt pretty clever for devising a solution, but the extra validation was even more encouraging.

Captain's Log, Airdate 170506

We Don't Need No Stinking Badges

Aircraft: MD-80

Crew: First Officer Shannon

We provided the only airline service at some of our stations, which has both advantages and disadvantages. One of the difficulties at these airports is with TSA. One day they came on board our aircraft to do a routine security search, but I heard something unusual as they introduced themselves to the cabin crew. I went back to check it out and the flight attendants said one of the TSA agents didn't have a badge. They had already begun their search, so I waited. When they were finished, I questioned them about it. There were two of them and one was obviously shepherding the other. He explained that she was new and, therefore, did not have a badge yet. This isn't that unusual and is acceptable as long as he was escorting her at all times.

My flight attendants quickly pointed out that this was not the real issue. They said she was using someone else's badge. I asked about it and he explained that she, indeed, was using a badge that belonged to someone else, but it wasn't like a "*badge* badge." She only used it as a key card to swipe through secure doors. *Huh?! Um, what?!* This was obviously a major security issue and I was stunned that they couldn't recognize it. If I did the same thing, I could end up in jail.

I told them to take me to their supervisor. We all went inside and the supervisor proceeded to give me the same explanation. At that point I stopped everything. Even though it didn't look like anything nefarious was happening, I wasn't going to let anybody go anywhere until I could get some acceptable answers. The issue was taken to the TSA regional office and to our company headquarters and the two groups worked it out. We went on our way but there was an eventual reprimand and retraining for those TSA agents.

Captain's Log, Airdate 180214

He's Still Running

Aircraft: MD-80

Crew: First Officer Jim

One of our constant challenges was flying to smaller airports. Fewer services are available, the runways tend to be shorter and we deal with wildlife more often. Our chief pilot once described our challenges as "aggressive flying" which required an equally aggressive approach to safety.

The most critical phase of flight for large, jet airplanes is on takeoff, especially for an MD-80. We often stretched the capability of our aircraft to the allowable limit. The main challenge is divided into two aspects balanced between the length of the runway: 1) get this 70-ton machine in the air before running out of available runway, but, at the same time, 2) plan for enough runway to stop if something goes wrong at the most critical point. Aborting a takeoff is rare, but insufficient respect for this second aspect has caused a number of accidents. With this in mind, airline training is geared toward continuing a takeoff once critical speeds are reached.

This was a typical night departure. We lined up on the runway and began the takeoff roll. Just after we reached 80 knots (one of those critical speeds that normally rules out aborts, except for critical failures), I saw an animal on the runway in front of us. It looked like a rabbit and I wasn't very concerned, but, as we closed the distance, I eventually saw that it was larger—a coyote. Unfortunately, and incredibly, he had decided to turn straight down the middle of the runway in his attempt to run away from us.

I was able to avoid the collision with the nose wheel and he went right under my feet just before we began to lift off. His next lethal threat was the left main landing gear and I was afraid there was no escaping it. After takeoff I reported it to the tower and suggested they send someone out to look for the victim. Damage to our landing gear was a possibility so I checked back with them after a few minutes to see what they had found. No dead coyote on the runway! We had straddled him, narrowly threading the deadly needle. He also somehow escaped the final threat of the hungry jet engines at full power passing over his head, although he surely would have been blown off his feet by the powerful jet blast.

This left me musing about this poor critter. He went out for an evening stroll only to be met with the biggest, fastest, loudest monster he could have ever imagined. It lit up the night sky and came chasing after him with a deafening roar and a powerful whirlwind that almost killed him as he was tossed around like a rag doll. None of his friends would have believed him.

When we got the report from the tower that he had survived the whole thing, I mentioned to Jim how crazy it was that he had decided to "run away" from us right down the runway. His response still makes me chuckle, "And he's *still* running."

Captain's Log, Airdate 170131

Barreling into My Airspace At 400 Knots

Aircraft: MD-80
Crew: First Officer Randy

Some airports are prone to the infamous "slam dunk" approach. Because of the proximity of mountains and/or airspace configuration, Air Traffic Control (ATC) will sometimes leave us higher than the normal descent profile. As pilots, we just have to figure out how to deal with it and this presents a challenge for big jets.

Descent planning for a large jet aircraft is part science and part art form. Too many pilots get lazy with this process and either end up descending too early or too late. Developing a plan that works out perfectly is a challenge I like to take on for each flight. When ATC places constraints on us that interrupt the normal planning, leaving us high, we call that a "slam dunk" approach. There are a couple of strategies to deal with it and I usually prefer the high-speed option. Aerodynamic drag on an airplane increases with speed. The high-speed option takes advantage of this by taking a steep descent angle and allowing the speed (and drag) to increase.

There are no regulatory speed limits at high altitudes, so the high-speed strategy is available up to the aerodynamic limit for the aircraft. We just have to leave room to slow down when we get down to 10,000 feet, where the speed limit is usually 250 knots (288 miles per hour). This is what I did on the descent today just like I (and many others) had done numerous times before. Apparently, the approach controller didn't like it, so he gave me a vector away from the airport when we checked on to his frequency at about 13,000 feet. This was not part of my descent plan. It was working out perfectly before he gave me the vector, so I questioned what it was for. His emphatic reply was priceless, "When you come barreling into my airspace at 400 knots, I have to do something." Randy and I both burst in to laughter. It's a good thing the controller couldn't hear us.

NOTE

Air Traffic Control (ATC) provides a valuable service and 99% of the interactions we have with ATC are positive. I have no intention of disparaging ATC in general for the very few negative experiences that I have had. Controllers are especially helpful when we face emergency situations.

Captain's Log, Airdate 170621

Radio Static

Aircraft: MD-80
Crew: First Officer Flynn

It was a typical summer afternoon with a lot of thunderstorm activity across the Midwest United States, but Flynn and I didn't note anything unusual. There were thunderstorms forecast right at our destination, so dispatch had filed an alternate with extra fuel as a contingency.

The flight was boring, but I was periodically keeping tabs on the thunderstorm situation. As we got closer and began planning the descent, the storm at the airport was not moving east as forecasted, so we discussed a possible diversion to our alternate. Our route took us directly over this airport and it was close to our initial descent point. With more than 30 minutes of extra fuel, we decided to hold right there at 33,000 feet and wait for the storms to clear. This strategy took advantage of the fact that jet engines burn a lot less fuel at higher altitudes. While circling overhead we listened to the recorded information broadcast to verify the weather and airport conditions were good at our alternate below us, in case the diversion was necessary.

As the fuel level approached a point that required a go/no go decision, we developed a strategy to extend our time window. Since the descent required about 100 miles (which happens to be the approximate distance between the two cities) we decided to initiate the descent toward our destination with the option to turn around half way down and return to our alternate if the weather did not improve during that time. This effectively gave us another 10-15 minutes for the thunderstorms to move to the east. It was a clever plan...

Unfortunately, as we descended below 20,000 feet and entered the clouds, static electricity started building up on our aircraft. This is a natural phenomenon familiar to anyone who has experienced a static shock between a fingertip and a metal surface. Most of us don't think much about the static buildup on a metal surface moving through the air, but it can get pretty strong when an airplane is moving so fast. Modern aircraft are equipped with static wicks that help dissipate the charge. The MD-80 has static wicks, of course, but on this particular aircraft, they were largely ineffective to the point that it affected our radios and they became unreadable with radio static. This was unexpected and we had not accounted for it in our plan, which led to a stressful dilemma: How was I going to communicate with Air Traffic Control (ATC) about a diversion if it became necessary?

Upon reaching our decision point, our onboard weather radar indicated the thunderstorm was still over the airport but continuing to move eastward, away from us. We were now faced with a difficult decision. The most conservative course with regard to our available fuel was to turn around but our compromised radios left us without a way to effectively communicate with ATC about the diversion. I could have transmitted "in the blind," declared an emergency and stated my intentions to divert but this option would have been rather dramatic. I would have done it if necessary, but I was hoping to avoid it. On the other hand, the expectation that the storm would keep moving eastward was convincing enough, so we pressed on.

We continued the descent and emerged from the "staticky" clouds at about 10,000 feet. The radios quickly returned to normal and we could freely communicate again, but our alternate was now beyond a comfortable reach. What we faced at that point was a few tense minutes during which we considered multiple options including declaring a low-fuel emergency. As it turned out, the thunderstorm did continue moving east and we were able to land without further delays.

Captain's Log, Airdate 171013

Are They Going to Arrest Me?

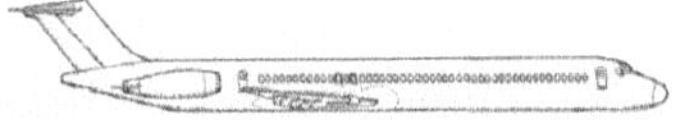

Aircraft: MD-80
Crew: First Officer John

Most of our flying was scheduled service but this trip was a charter flight. One of the challenges we faced in our charter operations was unfamiliar facilities and personnel, which sometimes lead to logistical breakdowns. Paperwork was the usual suspect. Dispatch would electronically send it to the station, but it wouldn't always get there. Such was the case on today's late-Saturday flight. Phone calls back and forth to dispatch didn't produce a solution, so the station agent escorted me into the office, where I stood next to the fax machine while the dispatcher made another attempt. I'm not sure why standing next to the machine made a difference but it worked. He then escorted me back out to the aircraft where we waited for the last of our fuel for the long flight across the country.

The agent who escorted me was also the tug driver who was set to push us back. I got all situated in my seat and then began a conversation with him over the headset as we waited for fuel. Within minutes, a police car pulled up next to the airplane. The exchange went something like this:

Me: What are the cops doing here?

Agent: They came to arrest me.

Me: No, seriously. What's up?

Agent: No joke. They want to arrest me for escorting you into the secure area.

Me: What? Are they going to arrest me too?

Agent: No. For now, they're saying just me.

At that point I looked up and saw a TSA agent standing directly across from me in the terminal, staring me down with a stern look and arms akimbo. We were the last flight to leave that evening, so TSA had closed the checkpoint once our people had been screened, but they usually hang around until the flight leaves just in case. Apparently, he had an issue with the agent escorting me to the office and back without TSA intervention. Ultimately nobody got arrested, but they did escort me off the aircraft and back to the security checkpoint, which they had reopened just for me. His ingenious solution was to take me outside security, then come back through the checkpoint for proper screening before I could return to my airplane. I felt so much safer after that and he felt more important as well.

NOTE

Transportation Security Administration (TSA) agents provide a valuable service and 99% of the interactions we have with TSA are positive. I have no intention of disparaging TSA in general for the very few negative experiences that I have had.

Captain's Log, Airdate 180107

Tornado Warning!

Aircraft: MD-80

Crew: First Officer Craig

It's unusual to have strong thunderstorms in early January but that was the forecast today. With marginal conditions, I like to keep tabs on the weather enroute. About an hour from landing, I checked in to see what we were dealing with. The report was calling for a tornado watch, so I called dispatch to see what his plan was. He told me that none of his weather reports, forecasts or radar indicated a problem. I probed him with questions because I wasn't interested in exposing my aircraft to a tornado. Beyond the obvious risk in flight, the aircraft would also be a sitting duck on the ground for a hungry twister. He insisted that everything was fine. I suggested we divert to the airport we were about to pass by to wait for the weather to clear but he was adamant that it wasn't necessary. We reluctantly decided to continue because we still had numerous options available.

About 40 minutes later and 30 miles from our destination, we got an urgent call from dispatch telling us to divert. A tornado was tearing through the local area! Fortunately we had enough fuel to turn around and go back to the airport we had suggested earlier. We diverted there where we loaded up on fuel and waited a couple hours for the storm to move on.

A wait like that is usually filled with a lot of activity—constant communicating with dispatch, crew and passengers, gathering information and evaluating options. Craig had an iPhone (still somewhat of a novelty at the time) which he used to get real-time radar information about the storm while we were on the ground. Prior to that night I had considered the iPhone just a toy with no practical value, but I was thoroughly impressed with the information Craig had at his fingertips, so I soon got one for myself.

What made this trip even more interesting was that my brother and his family were waiting for us at the destination. I called him a couple times to apprise him of our situation and give him updates. It was also useful for me to gather information from him about real-time airport conditions where he was. At one point they even had to take cover in the airport's tornado shelter. He obviously appreciated me keeping him in the loop, but the other passengers thought he was just blowing hot air. Here was this guy who would take a phone call and then claim that his brother was the captain of the flight, calling him with updates.

The storm passed after a couple hours and we got everything ready to continue. I called my brother one last time to let him know we were leaving shortly. It was a quick and easy flight and we didn't encounter any further weather difficulties. Everyone was obviously happy to see us and what a surprise for the doubters when I walked off the jetway and greeted my brother and his family!

Captain's Log, Airdate 180203

Min-i-mums

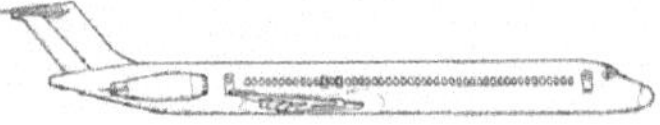

Aircraft: MD-80
Crew: First Officer Jim

Weather is sometimes less of a science and more of a guessing game. Professional meteorologists develop forecasts for each airport, which are substantially correct most of the time. Sometimes they're wrong; on rare occasions they're not even close. We try to err on the side of caution with any forecast, expecting it to be worse than predicted. If the conditions are worse than the accepted threshold, we make sure to carry enough fuel to make it to an alternate airport.

The weather at our destination for this trip was a bit marginal and the alternate was only about 30 miles away. I should have known better than to accept an alternate so close by, but the forecast looked good enough at both airports, so I took the bait.

Because of the nature of the situation I made sure to get an update about an hour before landing. Conditions were still okay at the destination but significantly worse at the alternate. It was no longer acceptable, so I called dispatch to have them find one that would work. The only good possibility he could find would stretch my current fuel supply to the legal reserve limit. If our approach was unsuccessful and we flew from there directly to the new alternate, we would land with just over 45 minutes of fuel remaining. This amount of fuel is legal but not very comfortable. Jim and I had a good discussion about it and I took the bait again because the conditions were still good enough and we were only about 30 minutes away. How much worse could it get?

The process of flying an instrument approach ends in one of two ways: 1) we see the runway, I call "Runway in sight" and we continue to a normal landing, *or*, 2) we arrive at the minimum altitude without seeing anything and I call "Minimums, negative contact." At this point, we would then execute a missed approach, climbing up and away from any hazards below. If the second case was our outcome tonight, we would then immediately divert to our distant alternate and arrive with the minimum 45 minutes of remaining fuel.

By the time we began the approach the cloud ceiling had fallen to the minimum limits and I was gradually feeling very uneasy about the looming potential diversion with the resulting fuel concern. Jim was flying this leg. As we descended lower and lower the tension was rising higher and higher!

The first positive indication is usually some type of feature on the ground that becomes visible through the fog, or "ground contact." We saw nothing as we approached the minimum altitude and I was beginning to regret the string of decisions that had led us to that point. As much as I didn't like the possibility, I was preparing to call "Negative Contact." We arrived at the prescribed altitude and

I called, “Min—i—mums. Neg—a. Runway in sight!” Jim’s steady hand (no “itchy” trigger finger) went right along with my drawn-out call. It was only by the slimmest margin, but we saw the runway and continued to a normal landing. What a relief!

Captain's Log, Airdate 180606

Brush with Disaster

Aircraft: MD-80

Crew: First Officer James

This flight was the closest brush with disaster that I've ever faced. It was a typical summer day with strong gusting winds bouncing us around, but there was nothing out of the ordinary as we began our approach to Runway 25 Left (R25L). James was flying the approach and I saw no indication to doubt his control of the situation as we closed the distance to the runway.

The first clue that something was unusual was our landing clearance which included a wind report: Newtown 427 cleared to land R25L, wind 160 at 7, gust 27. Gusting wind here is an everyday thing, but this combination was not. Runway numbers are based on their heading. Runway 25 indicates a heading of about 250°. Wind direction is given in the same terms. A "160" wind means it is coming from 160°. The math in this case meant that the wind was a direct crosswind of 90°. This is not unusual either, but the wind intensity really got our attention. It was blowing steady at about 7 knots (8 mph) but gusting to 27 knots (31 mph). The 20-knot difference is what concerned me. I thought about it for a few seconds and had a quick chat with James.

"Did he say *seven*, gust two-seven?"

"Yeah."

Again I considered the numbers, "Are you okay with that?"

He nodded and continued.

The wind really wasn't that bad as long as we didn't get that 20-knot gust at the wrong moment. Unfortunately, we did. Just as James started to raise the nose for landing, the airplane rolled sharply to the left. Adrenaline surged. Passengers screamed. My hands darted like lightning to the controls. By the time I got there, James had already turned the wings level. It all happened in just one extremely intense second. The landing from that point was perfectly normal.

I suspected that the wingtip might have touched the runway and the post-flight inspection confirmed just that. The landing light (which extends below the wing) and the fiberglass wingtip were broken, but the bigger concern was the slat (the front part of the wing that is extended forward and down for landing). A portion of it was ground off as it scraped along the concrete. It was very sobering to consider just how close we had come to a disastrous outcome.

James and I spent the next couple hours together as would be expected after such an incident. We had the opportunity to rehash what happened. At one point he admitted that he really wasn't comfortable with the reported wind, but he didn't want to admit it. I had to tell him that I had a huge problem with that. I had asked him specifically about it as we approached the runway and the response I got indicated that he was okay with it. Any hesitation from him would have been enough to prompt me to give up on that plan and simply use a different runway with more favorable wind. I don't know if he thought I would have looked down on him for it, but that certainly would not have been the case. As it was, I was thoroughly frustrated with him for not voicing his concern.

The FAA conducted a brief investigation and determined that it was simply an act of God—an ugly wind shear event with a heroic save. Neither one of us ended up with so much as a letter in our file. Our standards and training departments also did an investigation and determined we acted appropriately. In the end, there was nothing more than some damage to the aircraft and an opportunity to learn from the incident. I made the determination that, faced with similar circumstances, I would look the first officer in the eye and ensure that I clearly understood his comfort level (or lack thereof), while making it clear that I would be okay if he wanted to bail out and try something different.

Captain's Log, Airdate 190523

I Lost My Canopy

Aircraft: MD-80

Crew: First Officer Craig

Most communication with ATC is routine and mundane, but sometimes we hear something interesting. One of the most comical exchanges I've heard was about crew meals. Someone made a comment that touched off a flurry of responses from what seemed like everyone on frequency. Everybody had to add their two cents about their own plight with regard to crew meals or lack thereof.

DEFINITION

Canopy:
A plexiglass bubble that covers the cockpit of some aircraft. It opens and closes on the ground for entry and exit. It should be securely latched in flight.

The *strangest* exchange I ever heard happened on this flight. Somewhere over the Rocky Mountains a pilot declared an emergency and asked for vectors to the nearest airport, preferably an Air Force Base. The controller quickly gave him the requested assistance and then asked about the nature of his emergency. "I lost my canopy," was the response. Whoa!

The sector we were in was all high-altitude traffic, so this guy was above 30,000 feet. Craig and I looked at each other, questioning what we had heard. It was obviously a fighter jet, as evidenced by the "canopy." The transmissions did not have any air noise, indicating the pilot was inside a pressure suit/helmet. Still, it seemed like a crazy situation as I tried to imagine this guy flying along when, out of nowhere, the glass bubble between him and the upper atmosphere was suddenly gone. It had to be pretty chaotic but there wasn't a hint of stress apparent in his voice. He sounded like it was just another routine day at the office. Pretty impressive!

Captain's Log, Airdate 191106

Locked Out

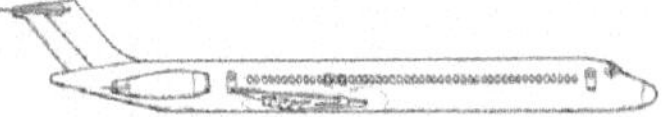

Aircraft: MD-80
Crew: First Officer Dave
Flight Attendant Mary

Dave had one of the most enjoyable personalities with which to work. It seemed like he was always in an amiable mood. He was also a good airman whom I could trust. The trip today took us to California, where the late fall weather was gorgeous. We quickly opened our windows after landing to enjoy the fresh air. I got out of the airplane and went into the terminal. Dave also decided to get out and enjoy the beautiful weather. Not long after that, the ground crew entered the cabin to assist a passenger with a wheel chair. The flight deck door made it difficult to negotiate the turn from the aisle to the exit, so Mary unlatched it from the open position to make more room. Click! The door quickly swung closed before anyone could catch it. The flight deck door was now securely locked with no one inside.

I found them grappling with the situation when I returned to the airplane. As great as the weather was, it had lured us both out of the flight deck and into a tough situation. They had tried to open the door with no success. The only remedy left was to climb through the window. Fortunately, they were both open. I volunteered for the difficult maneuver as a ladder was found and placed in position. Boarding at this station is done from ground level with a ramp, so my daring deed would be done in full view of the passengers who were waiting in line. Of course they stared and some laughed but it had to be done.

It's more difficult than it would seem to cross from a teetering stepladder into a small flight deck window, but I made it. I was the hero for the day as everyone was glad it worked out. Thank goodness for the mad skills and sense of balance I had developed climbing trees as a kid.

Captain's Log, Airdate 200111

Disappearing Runway

Aircraft: MD-80

Crew: First Officer Dave

There are some beautiful airports in the northern mountains of the United States. They're hard to beat as summer retreats, but the winters can be harsh. Tonight was cold and wet with a light breeze off the nearby lake—perfect conditions to develop fog in the area. Ground fog is an interesting phenomenon. It can be quite dense, with very low visibility, yet still shallow enough to be easily seen through from an airplane overhead. While everyone on the ground (inside the fog layer) can't see much, the view from above is not too bad.

When visibility is restricted, we use an Instrument Landing System (ILS) to guide us through clouds and fog along a precision flight path right to the runway. The first step of this system uses electronic guidance to arrive at a point where the approach lights can be seen through the fog. This series of lights then provides visual guidance to a point where the runway emerges to the pilot's view. The key at the end point of this system is to see the runway so that a safe landing can be made using visual references. If the runway does not come into view before the minimum altitude, a "missed approach" is executed that is designed to climb up and away from the obstacles below. It's an impressive system that has worked quite well for decades.

There was nothing unusual about the ILS approach tonight. ATC directed us to intercept the final approach course about 20 miles out and we could clearly see the runway lights from that distance. The airport was reporting one-half mile visibility, so we were expecting to descend into the fog layer, temporarily lose sight of the runway and then see the approach lights again before reaching 200 feet above the ground. This is the typical pattern in these conditions.

Despite our expectation, something strange happened on this particular approach. We descended lower and lower on the approach but not into the fog, never losing sight of the runway lights. We reached the minimum altitude and still no loss of visibility. At this point it appeared that the layer was so shallow that we would not lose sight of the runway. The half-mile visibility that the tower was reporting was either old or at some other part of the airport. I continued with a normal approach to about thirty feet above the runway. At this point I began the landing flare, slightly raising the nose to slow the descent rate and reducing the engine thrust to idle for a normal landing.

Poof! The runway was gone! There was a moment of disbelief then a very quick decision to make. When a jet engine is reduced to idle thrust, it takes a few seconds for it to spool up again. Nothing was going to prevent the aircraft from touching down at that point. I could attempt a "touch-and-go" (not something we ever trained for) or continue with the landing. I chose the latter. The main landing gear touched down and I saw two centerline stripes in front of me as I lowered the nose to the runway. This was the guidance I needed to continue the landing and avoid the precarious alternative. It was a strange situation that I had not seen before and hope I don't ever see again.

As we taxied to the gate, I couldn't help but wonder if the tower could see my tail sticking up above the fog layer like a shark fin above the water. The ground personnel were glad to see us because they had assumed that we would divert to somewhere with better visibility to wait for improvement. There was also a pilot from another airline who was waiting for us to give him a ride on our next flight. He approached me to ask if he could have a seat on our flight, expressing amazement that we were able to make it in with the current weather. He said nobody else had been able to do so for a couple hours and he was about to give up and call his company to report he would not be able to report to work that evening. It was fortunate for everyone that we had avoided the diversion, but it was only by the slimmest of margins.

Captain's Log, Airdate 200500

Open Fuel Panel

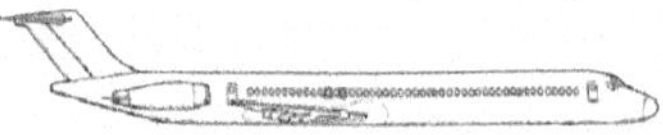

Aircraft: MD-80

When something is wrong, you never know who might have the most valuable kernel of information. It might be a flight attendant or a gate agent or a baggage handler. It might even be a passenger. It's vital to gather information from any source available so as to make the best judgement possible. To be sure, those with no technical knowledge can't typically provide useful observations, but it doesn't hurt to listen to what they have to say and evaluate it anyway. Accidents have occurred as a result of ignoring vital information that came from a source that the crew perceived to be uninformed.

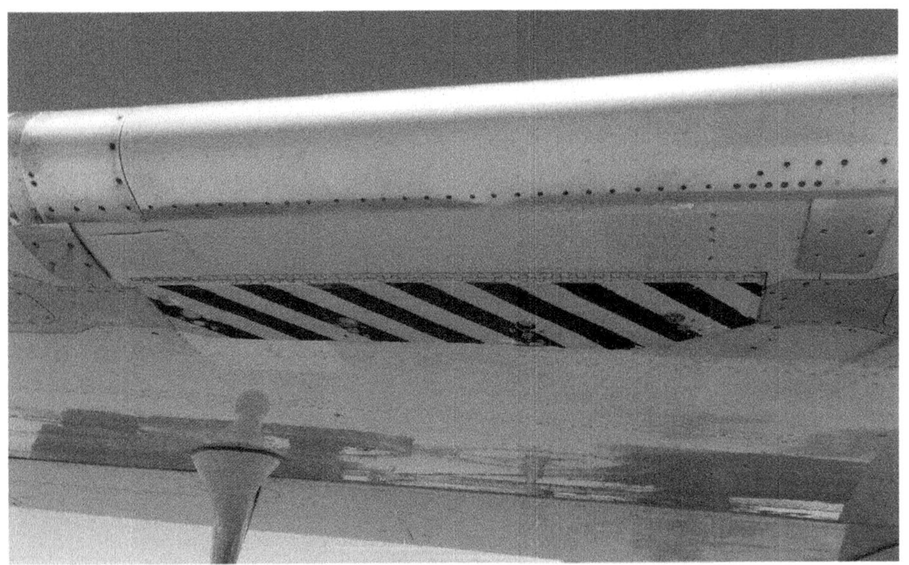

This yellow and black striped panel folds open to access the fueling controls.

Today we were almost done loading when a passenger approached me with a valuable bit of information. He said there was something unusual about a striped flap (see illustration) on the front of the wing that he had seen from the terminal window. He didn't know what it meant, but it *didn't look right to him*. I knew exactly what he was referring to and I thanked him for letting me know. It was the panel that folds down on the front of the right wing that allows access to the fueling controls. It was the fueler's responsibility to ensure the panel was closed after he was finished, but he had failed to do so. I had already done my exterior preflight inspection and there is no way to see that panel from the flight deck, so we could not have seen it. That observant passenger had given me a very helpful piece of information. The last line of defense would have been the ground crew, but it's never good practice to allow a problem to get to the last line. I went back outside and quickly closed and latched the panel. Problem solved!

Captain's Log, Airdate 200701

Fire!

Aircraft: MD-80
Crew: First Officer Tina

This was a typical summer afternoon and we were scheduled for two short round trips. After an uneventful first flight I was following my normal between-flight routine. I was in the terminal when my wife called. The smoke we had seen as I was leaving for work was the beginnings of a fire not far from our home. The blaze had destroyed Warm Springs Ranch, a beloved local recreation area. My parents were caretakers of the facility and their home there had been reduced to a pile of ashes. They were physically okay, but they had lost nearly everything and the fire was still not under control.

This was quite a shock! There was nothing I could do about it from where I was, but I needed to get back home. I called dispatch to let them know that after returning to our home base I would not be able to work the remainder of the trip. They went to work finding someone to replace me and I returned to the airplane. The preflight preparations were nearly complete. I was okay but my mind was racing and somewhat preoccupied.

Withholding information like that from fellow crew members would be terribly irresponsible, so I explained the situation to Tina. From that point on, she gladly took care of just about everything and did so impressively well. I did my duties as the captain, but she kept an eye on me and took charge of everything else. It was nice to have such a helpful partner in the flight deck with me that day. Her caring attitude and professionalism eased some of the stress I was facing until we got back and I was able to go home.

As far as my parents are concerned, all of their stuff was destroyed in the fire. The home they were living in was the caretaker residence. While that structure was destroyed, their personal home (several miles away) remained untouched. Fortunately, their insurance covered the replacement of all of the things they lost. Despite the trauma of the experience and the loss of everything that went up in smoke that day, they came out of the situation just fine. Even the recreation area was eventually rebuilt.

Captain's Log, Airdate 200731

Solar Oven

Aircraft: MD-80
Crew: First Officer Tina
Flight Attendant Eric
Flight Attendant Marcy

The MD-80 has an interesting history. It was originally designed and built by Douglas Aircraft in the late 1950s and early 60s as the DC-9. Douglas modified it in subsequent designs that stretched the length of the airplane. In the 1980s Douglas had merged with McDonnell Aircraft and a decision was made to also merge the latest technology with their old work horse. The result was a substantial redesign, which they designated the McDonnell-Douglas MD-80. Most of the changes were in technology integration into the existing design. While there were a few changes to the rest of the airplane, the systems remained mostly the same—a testament to its solid, sound, simple design. This process, however, led to a significant weakness in the air conditioning system: over time, the cabin grew longer, but the cooling system didn't keep up.

Almost everybody—crew or passenger—who has spent any time on an MD-80 in the summer understands this issue. The temperature in the cabin can range from annoying to almost unbearable. Operating the plane in hot environments doesn't help. I went to work each day expecting to end up soaked in sweat. We went to great lengths to mitigate the problem, but most afternoons were simply not comfortable until we could get the engines up to full speed and the airplane off the ground. Such was the case today as we prepared for a long slog.

Compounding the difficulty on this very hot day was a mechanical issue that forced us to switch to a different airplane that had been sitting out in the heat all day. The ground crew spent some time cooling the airplane before we started to board, but it was still about 80° in the cabin. We finally got everyone on board and got underway, but the line of airplanes in front of us meant it was going to be a long taxi. Fortunately, the slope of the taxiway was uphill, which helped to cool the cabin due to the increased engine power. I knew everybody on board was uncomfortable but the only solution to our situation was to get in the air as quickly as possible.

Ding! The flight attendants were calling to report a "puff of smoke" in the cabin. Smoke in the cabin is obviously a huge concern and could lead to an emergency evacuation. A decision about evacuation is among the most serious a crew can face. On one side is the *possibility* of fire and smoke inhalation, which can quickly become fatal; on the other is the virtual *assurance* that people will be injured if an evacuation is carried out. It is critically important to assess the situation as quickly and accurately as possible.

I was grateful to have Eric, a strong and seasoned flight attendant, on the other side of the flight-deck door. The simple fact that he was not struggling to speak was an indication that I had some time to quiz him about the threat. It turned out that the "puff of smoke" had only been small and had dissipated quickly. While this is not normal, an occasional drop of oil can escape through a seal and cause this very outcome. I advised him to keep a vigilant eye on the situation and let me know if anything got worse.

Ding! Only a couple minutes had gone by and I was concerned that the smoke had returned. This time the report was more an indication of the overall stress caused by the heat—someone was giving up and wanted to get off. At this point we had already advanced to number three in line and the ordeal with the heat was almost over. Surely this guy could wait just a bit longer. They tried to convince him, but he wouldn't have it. If we gave up our place in line it would be that much longer for all of us to get on our way. I told Tina to ask ground control for a few minutes to deal with the issue. They took us out of the line up to a holding spot.

At this point I was using the cabin inter-phone to talk with Marcy in the rear of the cabin and asked her about this guy who was so insistent. He was traveling with his pregnant wife and she was in distress. I certainly felt some compassion for him and his wife, so I wanted to talk to him myself. Marcy put him on the inter-phone and I tried to convince him that the ordeal was almost over, as we would be in the air shortly and the cabin would cool quickly. He continued his pleading to get off the airplane. As frustrating as it was, I couldn't hold them like prisoners. Dejected, I had Tina make the radio call for a return to the gate.

The way back to the gate was not easy because everybody else was waiting in line going the other direction. We were swimming against the stream. It was a long, circuitous route, but we started back and it was getting even hotter. I brushed off the increased heat because we were now taxiing down hill with the engines at idle power. We also wondered if it was just frustration that made us *feel* hotter. We finally made it back to the gate and Eric opened the flight-deck door. The temperature in the cabin had risen gradually and none of us had realized just how bad the situation was. Our daily exposure to the heat had blinded us somewhat to the plight of those who were not used to it. The scene was alarming!

The temperature had reached dangerous levels and most of the passengers were in distress. Gratefully, a riot hadn't broken out! The next few minutes, however, did became a bit chaotic as there was a scramble to help those who needed it most. Eric personally *carried* two people up to the terminal. The end result was a total of nine medical emergencies that were handled by paramedics. I cannot commend my crew enough for their handling of the situation, but it had taken its toll and none of us was in good shape. We were all pretty haggard. Eric was drenched in sweat, looking like he had just gone a few rounds with a gorilla.

This was one of the most stressful situations that I had faced and we wondered why it had gotten so unusually hot. Eventually the mechanics, who had begun working on the airplane, revealed our hidden nemesis. The puff of smoke that started the whole scenario had been the final gasp from one of our two air conditioning "packs." The internal turbine had seized. Without knowing what had happened, we proceeded with the long downhill taxi which only served to exacerbate the situation. I felt so bad that we were nearly cooking these poor people in a huge solar oven.

Captain's Log, Airdate 200912

Wing Tip, Windshield

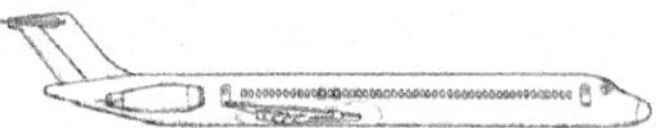

Aircraft: MD-80
Crew: First Officer Paul

It's very common for airline passengers to have a feeling of being "safe" when the airplane is on the ground. The challenge with ground operations, however, is that there are so many more things to hit and much tighter spaces in which to maneuver. The worst airline disaster in history happened on the ground. It's important for every crew to maintain at least as much vigilance on the ground as in the air.

It was late at night at the end of a long day. We had just landed and were on our way to the gate. As we came off the runway, ground control instructed us to turn right onto taxiway C and follow the aircraft ahead of us. As I turned on to C, the other airplane was just crossing C as it turned onto taxiway B. These two taxiways are parallel with the runway and both end up in the same place at the end of the runway. I put my finger on the radio transmit switch with the intent to point out the error, but then I thought, "Eh, no harm, no foul. Just let it go." Seconds later, the other crew realized their mistake and decided to fix it by turning back on to C. The problem with this move was that I had now moved along-side them and they were turning right into me.

We were seconds away from a collision as I abruptly applied the brakes. Paul had his head turned at the moment, but quickly snapped back as we came to a sudden stop. "What's wrong?"

I directed his attention to the wingtip of the other airplane that was precariously close to us. They had stopped as well, so now we were all waiting for ground control to make the next move. After a few seconds, I decided to break the silence and pointed out that the other crew had decided to come back to C. The controller chided him and he apologized. We all went on our way but that was a close one. Paul was impressed with what he called my "cat-like reflexes." Again, ground operations demand at least as much vigilance as flight operations.

NOTE

The worst ever airline disaster occurred in Tenerife (Canary Islands) in 1977. During takeoff, a KLM 747 collided with a PanAm 747 on the runway, killing over 500 people.

Captain's Log, Airdate 201223

Ghosts in the Fog

Aircraft: MD-80
Crew: First Officer Kelly

The weather was marginal due to low visibility and the passengers had been advised that we might have to divert. We always try our best to get them where they want to go, but weather conditions sometimes prevail, making it impossible. Electronic guidance can cut through the fog and get us close but, ultimately, we must see the runway in order to land on it. Having said this, I would never takeoff without a reasonable expectation of successful completion of the flight. Despite the low visibility, we expected to see the runway and land, delivering everyone where they wanted to go.

There was nothing unusual about this Instrument Landing System (ILS) approach. The visibility was reported as a half mile, which is the lower limit of what is allowed, so we needed to be sharp. I had flown with Kelly a number of times and always found him to be professional and proficient. It was his leg and he executed the approach quite well. As we descended closer to the runway, following the electronic guidance, I was starting to make out features on the ground below us. As we neared the "land or not" decision point, where visual contact with the runway is required, the familiar lights and shapes had materialized out of the fog, so I called, "Runway in sight." I heard Kelly respond and he continued the approach.

At this point, the approached turned unusual. As he transitioned from the electronic guidance to the visual picture in front of us, Kelly started "sliding" to the right. It was slow and subtle enough that I didn't say anything until after landing, but he had touched down on the right half of the runway. These paved strips are wide enough to allow for deviations off the centerline but it's still a matter of professionalism to put it right on the mark, which is exactly what I had seen Kelly do many times before. He quickly adjusted back to the line after touchdown, but it left me wondering what had happened, so I asked. His response was stunning, "I didn't really have the runway in sight."

This is exactly the reason why visual contact is necessary and I was frustrated that he hadn't let me know. It could have been much worse than simply missing the centerline. When I called the runway in sight, he responded and continued, which gave me every reason to believe that he could see it too. All he had to do was say something and the situation could have been quickly and easily addressed. I could have guided him for a few seconds to give him the orientation he needed or I could have simply taken the controls.

It's a big deal (and pretty rare) any time the captain takes the controls. It can bruise a pilot's ego. It's one of the worst things a first officer can experience—facing the idea that he couldn't handle it and the captain had to "save the day." While I completely understand this dilemma, there is no shame in not *seeing* something. On the other hand, not admitting it and putting everyone at risk is much worse and has no place in the crew environment.

Captain's Log, Airdate 211116

O Canada!

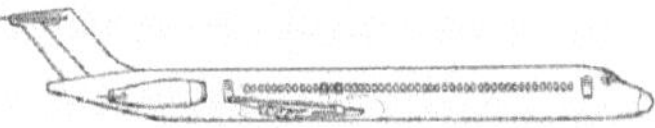

Aircraft: MD-80
Crew: First Officer Chase

I frequently flew charter trips across the United States and into Canada. It was fun and interesting because we flew to so many varied destinations. It was also a lot of work because the normal support system at each of our stations was not available. There were times we had to wear multiple hats. Sometimes the additional responsibilities created a very busy environment and anytime we went to an international destination it meant even more workload. This trip was almost a perfect storm of additional stuff to do.

The first leg of the trip was to Winnipeg, Manitoba (YWG) and the workload was mounting as we prepared everything we needed for the international flight. The long list of preflight concerns was filling my plate, so I handed some of them off to Chase as I dealt with the most pressing issues. The pace was demanding but we were able to take care of it all and push back on time. We took off into a beautiful autumn morning and headed north.

As we approached our cruising altitude it was time to take a break from the morning's crazy pace, right after I checked one last thing. Because of the marginal weather in YWG I wanted to take a quick look at the approach charts before I relaxed. Uh oh! No approach charts. This was one of the items on my preflight list that I had mentioned to Chase. I wanted him to check to make sure we had them before we left, but I had not made that clear, so it got overlooked. It would have been easy to blame him, but that would have been counterproductive. Besides, I was the captain and the ultimate responsibility was mine.

The universal truth is that anything behind us cannot be changed. Dealing with what lies ahead is the only real option available. The reality we had to face at the moment was going to an unfamiliar airport in challenging weather with no approach charts. This was a problem! We considered our options and briefly entertained the idea of continuing without them. This notion, however, was quickly dismissed as foolish. One of life's most important rules (and especially in flying) is not to compound one mistake by adding others on top of it.

The only sensible choice was to bite the bullet and admit my mistake. I called dispatch to inform them of our dilemma. There was no way to transmit the charts to us in the air, so we worked out a solution together. We would land in Bismarck, North Dakota (BIS), pick up the charts and then continue. It was an expensive and disruptive diversion, but the best option available under the circumstances. Then I had to admit my mistake to the flight attendants and explain our change of plan. The last step was to inform the passengers. I have never believed in lying to them, but this was a tough one. I explained to them that we were missing some paperwork and had to stop in BIS to pick it up before continuing into Canada. Everybody seemed to take it in stride. I admit I did leave out the part about it being my fault.

I learned an important and valuable lesson that day about delegation. Just mentioning the items to Chase was not enough. I needed to look him in the eye and say, "These things are your responsibility. Do not let us leave until they are taken care of. Will you do that?" Next would be to quickly note those items so as to check with him before leaving. Last would be to leave some kind of marker to remind myself.

At the end of the day, we got the job done and we were only a few minutes late. Obviously, it would have been better to avoid the diversion. It also would have been nice to avoid the difficult conversation with the chief pilot the next day. I simply took responsibility, apologized for the mistake and explained how I would avoid the same in the future. He didn't have a problem with that.

Captain's Log, Airdate 220114

Busy, Busy, Busy

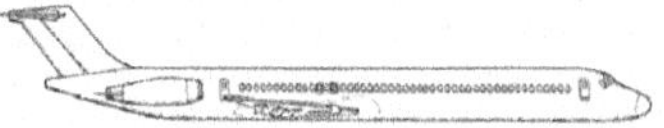

Aircraft: MD-80

Crew: Captain Mark

We frequently did long charter trips that exceeded our normal daily flight time limitations. These situations required an additional captain in order to split up the day so that each pilot (a total of three of us) would individually remain under the limit. This meant trading off during the day and sometimes a captain would end up in the right (first officer's) seat for a particular leg. This was the case today. It was my turn in the right seat for this short flight, with Mark in the left seat. Mark is a very good captain and we had flown together many times before.

These short flights were not unusual for this charter format as we would drop off one group and then fly empty to a nearby city to pick up another group. The short duration creates a somewhat demanding pace with everything that needs to happen in such a compressed amount of time. The standard division of workload in the flight deck is between pilot-flying (PF) and pilot-monitoring (PM). The PF flies the airplane while the PM monitors everything and handles all of the peripheral duties. PF tends to be the easier of the two roles, as long as nothing unusual arises. PM is normally the busier job, especially on a short flight. This was not unusual, however, and we were accustomed to the demanding pace. I thought I was getting off easy with the PF duties for this leg as I did not anticipate the unusual workload that was about to stretch my capabilities.

It was an ugly winter day in the Pacific Northwest with low clouds, ice and snow. The ground disappeared shortly after I lifted the aircraft off the runway as the gray winter clouds enveloped us for the very short hop. The icing started almost immediately. While this is not normally a big concern due to the reliable anti-ice capability of the MD-80, the intensity was demanding some attention.

Another difficulty was the airplane itself. Our company had acquired used airplanes from different carriers all over the world. While most of them were very similar, there were a few "odd" configurations. It was a part of the job that we laughed off most of the time, but today it was creating some extra workload. It also didn't help that I was in the right seat where things are a little bit different than what I was used to. I was busy but still managing it all until, "I'm off one." Mark was letting me know that he was switching to radio #2 to contact our station personnel for gate information. "I've got one," was my response indicating that I would handle Air Traffic Control (ATC) on radio #1 while he was off.

For some reason the station call took more time than normal and I was mostly on my own in the meantime. Then ATC started to pile on additional requests. The heading and altitude changes were pushing me to a point of "task saturation" as I tangled with the "oddball" flight guidance in this particular airplane. Saturation can be a big problem if critical items start to slip through the cracks. It took everything I had as an airman to stay on top of the situation. It required intense focus on the most important aspects. I might have missed a call or two from ATC, but I managed to get the airplane stabilized on the approach as Mark rejoined me in the battle. The landing that followed was anti-climactic, but that flight was one of the busiest I've ever had.

In hind sight, the right thing to do—the smart thing—would have been to admit I was getting buried and ask Mark for help. The call to the station was not a critical task and could have waited until after landing. The temptation to be the hero was alluring and almost pushed me to the point of overload. This is one of the important reasons for having two qualified crew members in the flight deck. Ultimately, it worked out, but it would have been better for me to swallow my pride and let Mark know I was reaching my limit.

Captain's Log, Airdate 220214

Douglas Drenching

Aircraft: MD-80
Crew: First Officer Manny

Another little quirk about the MD-80 is the Douglas Drip. Each of the pilot's side windows slide open for various useful reasons. The mechanism that opens and closes these windows is quite an engineering feat. I suppose it worked well when it was new, but the old, worn-out version usually doesn't seal very tightly. The design relies heavily on the cabin pressurization system to complete the seal after takeoff by pressing the window tightly against the frame. On the ground, however, the window seals were notoriously leaky in the rain—the Douglas Drip.

This trip included a short overnight. We parked the aircraft and left it in the drizzly rain for the night. When we returned in the morning, we found the typical "puddles" and mopped them up before we got started. My window was leaking enough that I put quite a few paper towels in strategic spots to catch the continuing drips.

There was nothing else unusual as we prepared, boarded and pushed off the gate. We taxied out to the runway and, as we neared the end, I slowed down to make the turn. Suddenly the floodgates let loose! I don't even know where all that water came from, but the drip turned into a gush and my lap got absolutely soaked. It was a Douglas Drenching! I just sat there in stunned disbelief. It would have been easy to get upset about it, but Manny started laughing. He was cracking up about my ridiculous plight. Life can be rather grim if you can't step back and laugh at yourself. It was the only sane choice I had at the moment.

Even though I would like to have thrown in the towel (pun intended), I sucked it up and we continued. Sitting like that for over four hours in my wet, cold seat was not pleasant but I survived. Barely! At least I was dry enough by the time we arrived home that I didn't elicit strange stares when I got off the airplane.

Captain's Log, Airdate 220416

I See Dead Pets

Aircraft: MD-80
Crew: First Officer Barron

Whenever so many people are brought together in such a small space, the potential for strange things to happen is almost guaranteed at some point. Even considering all of the unusual things I've seen over the years, this case was exceptional.

It was Monday and the trip included a short round trip to a not-too-distant station, like every other Monday that month. After boarding was complete for the first segment, the flight attendants brought a concern to me about a dog. A sweet little old lady was traveling with her pet. All of its paperwork was in order, but it looked and sounded very sick. We conferenced together as a crew about what to do. The flight attendants decided they could accommodate her and the dog since they were already on board and it was only a short flight.

I can't say it was pleasant, but the flight attendants did what they could to make the best of the situation. They took care of the lady and her dog while attending to everyone else on board as well. We arrived at our destination with no further concerns and everybody was glad it had worked out. We moved on and went about the rest of our day.

The following Monday brought us back to the same trip again. At this point seven days had passed. I had flown ten separate flights, logging more than 21 hours of flight time and covering over 7,000 miles. My different crews and I had served over a thousand passengers. The flight from the previous week was a distant memory.

As we prepared to board the return flight of that same trip, the gate agent passed along a report from TSA that someone was trying to bring a dead dog on the flight. My reply was an emphatic NO. There was no way we were going to take a dead dog on board our aircraft. As we talked about it, we started to remember the situation from the previous week. We wondered aloud if it could be the same lady. At this point all kinds of unpleasant ideas crept into our collective imagination. Had the dog died and she was actually attempting to take it back home? Yuck!

Anyone who has played the telephone game in which a message is passed from person to person is familiar with the crazy outcome. The message typically changes with each new person who relates it and the resulting tale is astonishingly different. This situation was a good illustration. It was indeed the same lady from seven days before and the poor dog had actually died. The key piece of information missing from the original report was that she had cremated her dear pet and its ashes were safely secured in an urn. This was obviously a *huge* difference and we welcomed her back on board.

Captain's Log, Airdate 220802

Please Don't Fail!

Aircraft: MD-80

Crew: First Officer Gary

The Douglas engineers created a rather innovative solution for the MD-80 called the "optimum flap" system. The standard flap setting for takeoff is 11 degrees, but the airplane is certified to takeoff with any flap setting from 0 to 24 degrees. The basic principle for this system is a trade-off. Higher settings require less runway but result in decreased climb performance after liftoff. On the other hand, lower settings require a higher speed and more runway but allow the aircraft to climb better after takeoff.

Summer time temperatures at hot airports often require a flap setting less than 11 degrees for takeoff because of the decreased climb performance. The longest runway at this airport is almost three miles long, which allows enough room for very low flap settings and very high speeds (over 200 mph) on takeoff. This requirement often led to exhilarating (not in a good way) adventures on takeoff. Approaching the end of the runway at that speed was never one of my favorite things. I used every trick I could devise to avoid the situation, but sometimes the laws of physics demanded it.

The airplane was very heavy for takeoff on this hot afternoon. The performance calculation required a flap setting of two degrees and there was no way to avoid it. I lined up with the runway and handed the controls off to Gary for takeoff. We started the long roll down the runway and I counted the distance-remaining markers as we accelerated—five thousand, four thousand, three thousand. It took more distance than it should have. The cause for this could have come from any number of different factors but it didn't matter at the moment. We had reached the point of no return and Gary lifted the lumbering machine into the air. The first public road runs right along the edge of the airport property. I noted the cars driving below us as we crossed over it at less than 100 feet and over 220 mph.

Having cleared the first obstacles, the next pressing concern was the rising terrain ahead of us. We were easily climbing faster than the terrain ahead, but my concern was about the engines. All transport jets are certified to be able to climb out of trouble with only one engine running, but I was hoping—and praying—that I would not have to test those requirements at the moment. If one of the engines had failed, I'm not sure what would have happened. "Please don't fail!" I silently prayed over and over until we reached the point where the ground clearance was comfortable again. There's almost nothing that raises my level of concern in an airplane to "scared," but this situation had produced a spike of adrenaline that had me worried for a minute or two. Gary made a turn to the east and we continued on our way. As we climbed through about 7,000 feet, I took a deep breath and said, "I gotta be honest, Gary. That was kinda scary." We were both relieved it was behind us.

Captain's Log, Airdate 230405

Stop!

Aircraft: MD-80

Crew: First Officer Dave

There are so many things that can go wrong with an airline operation. It's amazing to me that it works most of the time. This list of things does not refer to safety-related concerns, which are always the highest priority. No flight crew would ever knowingly accept unwarranted risk with any operation. What the list does include is all the other hundreds of moving parts and pieces of the system that must come together in harmony to ensure an acceptable level of reliability and on-time performance. It's yet another testament to human achievement that the traveling public takes this complex choreography for granted. It comes together most of the time (for me, about 90%). We all know the frustration that arises when it doesn't. The problem is that it sometimes only takes one small slip for the whole system to screech to a halt.

The trip sequence for today was four short legs. The weather was good at all of our destination airports and everything was right when we arrived early on the first leg. It was a bright spring day with a good airplane and a good crew. We stopped at the gate and the jetway pulled up to the aircraft. One very small problem came up while opening the door. There wasn't enough room for the door to swing all the way open. This happens occasionally with MD-80s because the door swings so far forward. We simply needed the operator to back up, reposition the bridge a few inches toward the front of the airplane and then come back in place. She accidentally went the wrong way! Instead of backing up, she went forward, driving the platform into the side of the airplane. I immediately yelled for her to stop but the damage was already done.

We inspected the side of the airplane to assess the damage. The dent was small but in a terrible spot. Airplanes collect small dings over time and most are inconsequential. The concern with this one was its location along a rivet line. The underlying structure might have been damaged, requiring an inspection from inside the cabin. Unfortunately, that part on the inside was behind the forward lavatory, which would have to be removed to fully evaluate the damage. A mechanic was called and he confirmed the disappointing diagnosis: the airplane could not continue.

FUN FACT

Old regulations allowed for a sixteen-hour duty day. New rules have since curtailed this to a less-fatiguing limit that is based on multiple factors.

Just one small slip had torpedoed the rest of our day. The passengers for the remaining three flights would now be hours late and our workday would stretch past fifteen hours. The next several hours became airport appreciation time as we got to explore the terminal and its back rooms while dispatch rounded up another aircraft and crew. By the time we got under way again, the whole four-leg sequence was no longer possible. We did the second and third legs but had to spend the night there before completing the final leg the next day.

The crew that ferried the airplane to the repair facility had to do so unpressurized due to structural concerns. Nobody wanted to test the high stress of pressurization on the damaged area until the lavatory could be removed and expert eyes could evaluate it. This limited their altitude to 10,000 feet and ruled out crossing over any mountains. They were forced to take a circuitous route along the coast of California instead.

It was just one of those rare days that nobody wants to deal with, but we had to play the hand we were dealt. We all made it work the best we could and it was nice to have a great crew helping each other as we tackled it together.

Captain's Log, Airdate 230502

Rudder Heat

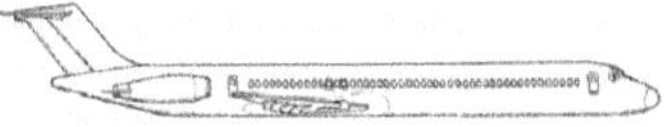

Aircraft: MD-80

Crew: First Officer Mike

Mechanical problems are always annoying and sometimes rather frustrating. Today it was a case of going from one end of the scale to the other. During the initial climb, I heard a click—the familiar sound of a circuit breaker (CB) tripping. No caution lights came on, so it wasn't a high priority in my mind. The panel behind us had dozens of individual CBs, so I waited until it was convenient to check it. What I discovered was the rudder-limiter heat CB was the culprit.

Circuit breakers are very important safety devices. If any particular electrical circuit draws too much current (usually because of a short somewhere), the CB automatically cuts it off, providing a large measure of protection from an inflight electrical fire. It's possible to reset a tripped circuit breaker, but it's generally not a good idea. Trying to recover whatever component or system lost is rarely worth the risk of a fire.

Most large jet airplanes have a system that limits the travel of the rudder at high speed to avoid over-stressing the airframe. An integral part of this system is the probe that senses aircraft speed. This probe is heated with an internal electrical element to prevent any ice accumulation on it in flight. The circuit for this element is what had tripped the CB.

I called dispatch and we strategized together about how to deal with the problem. As long as we didn't encounter any icing conditions, the system would not be needed. The forecast indicated that the weather system extending between us and our destination would continue its move to the east, allowing a descent clear of any icing. We continued based on this assessment. If the forecast didn't pan out, the contingency plan was to divert to an alternate airport. It was a good plan, but the weather did not move as expected. We entered a holding pattern above the alternate, keeping tabs on the weather there to make sure it was still available. We continued holding as long as our fuel would allow, but that stubborn system refused to keep moving east as forecast, so the diversion became necessary.

The stop at the alternate was only intended to be an hour or two. We would take on more fuel there and continue as soon as the weather moved. We waited a while, but that relentless system didn't budge. After hours of waiting, we reached our legal time limit for the day and had to throw in the towel. Dispatch sent a rescue airplane that did not have any icing limitations, and that crew continued the flight with our passengers. It turned out to be such a frustrating day over what seemed like such a small problem.

Captain's Log, Airdate 230628

I Totally Lost It

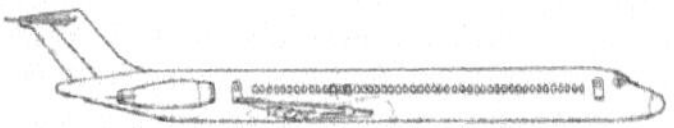

Aircraft: MD-80
Crew: First Officer Scott

Regulations at the time set a limit of eight hours of "flight time" in a single day. This measurement only includes the time from push back to arrival at the destination gate, so it's not unusual for those eight hours to turn into twelve plus hours of total time on duty. That can make for a very long day. Two of these days back-to-back with minimum rest in between can sometimes push a guy to the edge. At least for me it did.

After two very long days of fighting operational challenges and scorching heat, we were both reaching our limits. The MD-80 does have "air conditioning" but most of its effectiveness comes after the engines are at full power. Since taxiing with full power is impossible, our lot was to simply suffer in the heat until after takeoff. The return to our home base tonight was the last of four legs for the day, eight legs over two days. It was late at night as we lined up for the familiar approach 25 miles out. The runway lights were signaling the end of our two fatiguing days, a beckoning light at the end of our long, difficult tunnel.

Keeping a mental picture of all the other aircraft around you is an important skill. Air Traffic Control is responsible to sequence arrivals to the runway, but pilot awareness of the position of other traffic in the area provides some anticipation of the controller's plan. It's normally very predictable and maintaining the picture helps to avoid surprises. We were aware of an aircraft out ahead of us going the opposite direction. The most obvious place in the sequence for them was to turn in front of us on the approach, so I started slowing down to ensure adequate spacing.

As they turned in front of us, the spacing was coming together perfectly and I was patting myself on the back for such good planning. Then the controller did something unexpected and ridiculous. He cancelled our approach clearance and told us to turn 90 degrees right over concern for inadequate spacing. Not only was it unnecessary and counterproductive, but the surrounding mountainous terrain made it reckless. The turn pointed us directly toward one of those mountains. His impetuous move made no sense, it blew up my perfect planning and, worst of all, he had just stolen the light at the end of our tunnel.

I lost it! The pent-up frustration and fatigue of the last two days *exploded* all over the flight deck and it was not pretty. Fortunately, my rant was contained between the two of us, where the controller could not hear it, or I certainly would have been in trouble. Scott was not only my first officer but a good friend. He instinctively knew the answer to my explosion was laughter. Laughing at me was exactly what I needed at the moment to snap me back to my senses. I was still upset but at least I had regained my composure enough to talk to the controller.

With all the professionalism I could muster, I calmly chided him for his ridiculous decision to point me at a mountain in the dark. He asked what I wanted. "Whatever will get me on the ground the fastest," was my terse reply.

"I can get you to Runway 19 Left."

I snapped back, "I'll take it."

"Okay, cleared visual approach Runway 19 Left."

Ultimately, I'm not proud of what happened that night. I wish I had maintained my composure. When we finally got to the gate, I apologized to Scott. He said, "Other than my ears are bleeding, I'm okay." It was a good lesson for me. Since then, I've focused on recognizing the signs of stress that can lead to such an explosion and deal with it before it reaches a boiling point. I'm confident that the same situation today would produce a much more restrained response. I'm really glad that my friend Scott was there to talk me—laugh me—off the ledge.

Captain's Log, Airdate 231121

Four Suspicious Guys

Aircraft: MD-80

Some stations just seem to be the center of strange. Today I was sitting at the gate, just about ready to depart, when the gate agent came in to give me what I thought was routine information. Instead she whispered in my ear, "You have four suspicious guys onboard." I thought she must have been joking, but the look on her face indicated otherwise. I got off the airplane to talk with her privately and find out why these guys were on my airplane. She directed me to the cops who were at the gate checking on this group.

The officer explained the situation. They were watching a suspected drug house when these guys showed up. They went in empty-handed, came out with duffel bags and drove straight to the airport. This obviously drew suspicion and the police thought they were about to nab these guys with either drugs or cash or both. They worked with TSA agents to thoroughly search their carry-on bags but found nothing. The last thing they were checking was to make sure they didn't have any checked bags. While this was an interesting story, I wanted to know why these guys were on my airplane. He understood my concern, but he pointed out that they had not committed any crimes, so there was nothing they could do.

That was not what I wanted to hear but I returned to the aircraft and explained the situation to the lead flight attendant. Her reply was impressive, "Yeah. I know which guys you're talking about. We'll keep an eye on them." Ultimately that was it. They behaved themselves during the flight and I have no idea what happened after that. It made me wonder if they were just a decoy or if they were doing a dry run to test what law enforcement would do about it.

Captain's Log, Airdate 240303

Is This a Check Ride?

Aircraft: MD-80
Crew: First Officer Don

This was a very unusual day. Most of my days during this time period were dedicated to the training department. I rarely got a chance to fly, because I was either in a classroom or simulator teaching other pilots. This trip was my first day of flying in almost three months. This is not insignificant, because pilot skills are perishable. Of course teaching other pilots keeps my head in the game, but it's not the same as actually doing it myself. Neither would this be an easy, routine day. Our destination was a great airport for training in small airplanes, but operating an MD-80 there was challenging. The weather was also a challenge with snow flurries and low cloud cover.

We reviewed the dispatch release and weather briefing for the flight. Based on this information, we were expecting about 2 miles visibility at our ETA. This required an alternate, but we were still expecting to make it to our destination without any problems. We took plenty of fuel to complete the flight plus divert to the alternate, if necessary, and a little extra for other contingencies. Dispatch contacted us about an hour before landing to let us know that our company aircraft had just landed and reported 2 miles visibility and braking action on the runway was good. Everything was coming together nicely.

I briefed Don on the details of the Instrument Landing System (ILS) approach to Runway 35 Left (R35L). The most significant challenge we faced was a slight tail wind on landing. A tail wind requires more landing distance and this airport's longest runway was a bit short, but our calculations showed that we had plenty of room. One detail that we both had missed was that the ILS to R35L was out of service. Once we got in range we listened to the ATIS broadcast and discovered our oversight. We then discussed the next best alternative, which was the VOR approach to Runway 17 Right (same runway, opposite direction). A VOR approach does not afford the same level of precision nor does it give any vertical guidance for the descent. These factors mean that more visibility is required in order to see the runway with enough time to safely maneuver for a safe landing. We still did not consider this to be a problem because the visibility was 2 miles and the tailwind would now be a headwind. While a successful approach was expected at this point, we discussed a possible diversion if we couldn't see the runway.

DEFINITION

ATIS:
Automatic Terminal Information Service. A radio broadcast that includes weather and other useful airport information. It's recorded and usually updated every hour.

An instrument approach is an amazing thing to see. It guides the pilot to a landing position without the need to see any references on the ground. At some point during the approach, features on the runway gradually materialize out of the surrounding white or gray "soup" and, assuming it all looks right, a normal landing follows. We descended through the snow and fog until we could see features on the ground below but no runway. We continued to the point where a "missed approach" was required without seeing the runway, so I pushed the thrust levers forward and began to climb. Seconds later I got a glimpse of the runway. It was nice to see it, but a safe landing could no longer be made with so little room to descend so I continued to climb. It was disappointing but our only choice now was the diversion we had discussed.

As we climbed up and away from the ground and headed toward our alternate, things got interesting. The controller reported that the ILS was now working and we could use that approach. Normally I would consider this a trap to get lured into a futile second approach. We had just seen the runway, however, so we fully expected that an ILS approach (which would allow a lower descent and a closer look) would be successful. We briefly discussed our options and decided we had enough fuel that would allow the extra attempt, so we took the bait, leveled off and turned around.

DEFINITION

VOR:
VHF (Very High Frequency) Omnidirectional Range. A navigational beacon that has been the workhorse of radio-based navigation for decades.

This would require quick action to get everything set up for the new approach in a compressed time frame. Normally we avoid situations that force us to rush, but the limited fuel supply left us with less time than I would have preferred. We had also already discussed this approach earlier in the flight, so it didn't seem to be too big of a concern.

As luck would have it, not long after we made the turn and began the descent, my flight guidance computer went off line. Computer #2 was still available with normal indications on Don's side, so I handed the controls to him. Given our intention to divert, I had already flipped my book to those approach charts (paper approach charts, how primitive!), so I quickly flipped back and set up my radios for the ILS approach to Runway 35L.

Something else was now wrong! My instruments were not receiving the ILS signal. I vocalized my concern and we began to work the new problem. In the meantime, my flight guidance computer had come back on line, so I took the controls again. I quickly discovered that the problem was my mistake. In my haste, I had flipped through my book to the airport just one page prior which had a similar name and also happened to have an ILS to Runway 35. I quickly corrected the error as we continued toward the runway at over 200 miles per hour.

Now that I was all set up, I could see that we were way too high, so I had to make an aggressive descent to recover. This would not have been acceptable if we were too close to the ground but given our altitude above 5,000 feet, I had enough room to make it work. I intercepted the electronic glide slope and took a deep breath. Everything that had brought us to that point had been challenging but now it was just a simple ILS. Piece of cake!

We continued the descent out of the snow and clouds until we could see the runway just as we had expected, about one mile out. New problem! Now that we could clearly see the runway, we could also clearly see that it had not been plowed. It was covered with fresh snow. I was rather irritated to find that the airport personnel had not been diligent with snow removal. Now we had only a few seconds to assess the situation and make a judgement. Again, we had already briefed this approach earlier, so we had a basis for a good decision. Even with a slight tailwind, we had previously determined that it was within limits. We also knew that our company

MD-80 had landed about an hour earlier and reported good braking action on the runway. We decided to continue.

After all that, the landing was anticlimactic as the aircraft decelerated nicely and we stopped with plenty of room to spare. I couldn't remember ever having so many things go wrong all at once. It seemed like a check ride with a ruthless check airman trying to see how many problems he could pile on us to see if we could handle it. Wow!

Captain's Log, Airdate 250614

Just Coasting Along

Aircraft: MD-80
Crew: First Officer Jaime

Fuel planning is a critical preflight task. Carrying enough fuel (with additional safety margins) is essential, but carrying too much fuel is very expensive. The challenge of striking the correct balance between the two for each flight falls jointly upon the captain and the dispatcher. We carefully calculate how much fuel is needed, relying on regulations, policies and experience to account for any potential pitfalls, then usually add a little bit more for "mom and the kids." This process almost always yields enough fuel to successfully complete the flight, but unforeseen circumstances can sometimes foil the best plan and leave us short. One of these is the extended pre-takeoff taxi delay.

The typical taxi time before takeoff at our home base is 10 to 20 minutes. Taxi delays are significant when considering the rate of fuel consumption for jet engines. An MD-80 can burn 2,000 pounds

(300 gallons) of fuel every hour *before* takeoff. One way to stretch the fuel supply is to only start one engine for use during taxi and then start the other one just before takeoff. We did this today because of an unanticipated delay caused by thunderstorms in the area. Long departure delays are not very common at this airport, but this was one of the worst I had seen and it was threatening to stretch beyond the fuel we had available. Several aircraft in the line-up had already thrown in the towel and returned to the gate for more fuel. This is particularly galling because you lose your place and have to start over again at the back of the line.

Another strategy to stretch the fuel is to pull off into a waiting area and shut down both engines. In this case the Auxiliary Power Unit (APU) is used for electrical power and air conditioning. The APU uses much less fuel than the engines do. Our route to the runway today was on taxiway C, which did not have any waiting areas but did offer something even more useful—a downslope. At one point we were obliged to stop for several minutes on the taxiway, so I decide to try something I had never done before. I shut down my only running engine, hoping that gravity would allow us to coast along when it was time to move again. It worked. When the time came, I released the brakes and the slope was just barely enough to get us rolling again behind the aircraft in front of us. Our efforts paid off in the end, as we were able to make it to the runway with just enough fuel to safely complete the flight. I couldn't help but pat myself on the back for finding a way to make it work out.

DEFINITION

APU:
A smaller-size jet engine located inside the tail. Its purpose is to produce power and pressurized air for various purposes such as air conditioning.

Captain's Log, Airdate 250707

Can't See Anything

Aircraft: MD-80

Crew: First Officer Eric

The weather was marginal, with drizzling summer rain. Normally we need about a half mile visibility and the forecast was calling for 2 miles, so we weren't really concerned about having to divert to our alternate. Even though we were confident the weather wouldn't be a problem, we still checked on it with about an hour left in the flight. Unfortunately, the conditions had worsened and the visibility was now at our limit of a half mile. The good news was the approach to Runway 2 met the requirement for slightly lower visibility. It is equipped with specialized equipment called Runway Visual Range (RVR) that measures the visibility more accurately and reports it in hundreds of feet. The minimum visibility for this approach was 1800 RVR (slightly less than a half mile) so we still felt good about our chances of success for the approach.

When the visibility gets really low, we rely on the approach lights to help us transition from the electronic guidance to the visual markings on the runway. If we don't see the approach lights by the time we reach the minimum altitude, we simply execute what is called a missed approach and quickly climb to a safe altitude per the prescribed procedure.

As we checked on with the final controller, he informed us that the visibility was reporting 1800 RVR. Now we were concerned about the success of the approach. There was still a chance we would be able to see the lights, but only by the narrowest margin. I requested that the approach lights be turned up to the highest brightness to increase our chances. He confirmed they were indeed set at the upper limit and we attempted the approach. An instrument approach in low visibility is an amazing thing to see. We follow the electronic guidance to a point where the visual world gradually materializes out of the gray nothingness surrounding us. The first sign is usually some kind of features on the ground, such as buildings or trees. In this case we saw absolutely nothing as we reached the minimum altitude, so I initiated the missed approach.

We had some extra fuel to work with before we would have to divert, so we entered a holding pattern. While we circled, the visibility began to improve. It steadily came up to 2600 RVR so we decided to try the approach again. Our chances of seeing the lights were now pretty good and we were confident we would be landing soon. As we descended to the minimum altitude for the second time, I was amazed that nothing was materializing out of the mist. Once again we were frustrated and I had to execute the missed approach.

At this point our extra fuel was used up and we had no choice but to divert to our alternate. As we made our way that direction, we discussed what went wrong because this was certainly unusual to not see *anything* on the approach. We wondered if there was possibly something wrong with our instrumentation. We landed at the alternate airport and put on a bunch of extra fuel to get ready for another attempt to complete the planned flight. The weather was improving, so I intentionally dragged my feet to allow it to improve even more. The reported visibility eventually improved to 1 mile, so we were now very confident it would work. We took off again and headed back to our destination. Again we checked on with the approach controller and this time he reported the RVR had risen to 5000 RVR. This was now going to be a no-brainer.

We started our third attempt and I again requested the approach lights be turned up to the maximum brightness, but once again we were surprised that the approach lights were not visible. As we approached the minimum altitude for the third time, I was in absolute disbelief that we still couldn't see the lights. I was just about to push the "Go-Around" button again when Eric said, "Approach lights in sight." Then he added the strange comment, "The lights are not on but I can see the structure." *What!?*

We continued to the landing, but I was stunned—and livid. This whole mess was caused by bad approach lighting. Once we were clear of the runway, I reported the outage. The controller replied that his system showed the lights working just fine. I replied, "I was just there looking at them. They're not on." Not only did they fail, but the monitoring system also failed. What an expensive and disruptive mess as a result! We were only one of several flights that diverted to other airports that day. Grrrr!

Captain's Log, Airdate 250720

That's a Lot of Work

Aircraft: MD-80

Crew: First Officer Scott

I was temporarily assigned to Los Angeles, California (LAX) as my base for the month. I was glad to be out of the summer heat at our home base, but I had to commute back and forth to LAX every week. Most of my traveling was on the jump seat of whatever airline could accommodate me and this week offered something interesting as I watched the crew in front of me doing their job.

Most big airports have STAR (Standard Terminal Arrival Routing) procedures that help to keep all the pilots and controllers on the same page in a demanding environment. LAX is well known for its complex STARs because of the mountains and numerous airports in the area. Automation helps a great deal to reduce the workload, but this particular airplane was not equipped with some of the latest, most useful technology. As I watched the crew meet all the requirements for the STAR without the automated systems, I was impressed and couldn't help but think to myself, "Wow! That's a lot of work." I was grateful that the MD-80 *did* have the equipment that made my life easier.

The next day I flew my trip as scheduled, but something was wrong with the airplane. The auto-throttle system, one of the most useful pieces of automation, was broken. The MD-80 can fly just fine without the auto-throttles and there are procedures that allow us to continue when certain things are broken, but it does create a lot more work for the crew. Now the tables were turned, as I had to meet all the requirements for the STAR on the return flight to LAX. It was a deja vu moment: I couldn't help but consider the irony of the flight from the day before and think, "Wow! This *really is* a lot of work." I was just glad I didn't have to deal with it every day.

Captain's Log, Airdate 250729

Wake Turbulence

Aircraft: MD-80
Crew: First Officer Troy

One of the most concerning hazards we face is what is known as wake turbulence. Every airplane creates a wake behind it the same way a boat does in the water. The bigger the aircraft, the more powerful its wake. In order to mitigate the risk, the FAA has designated a separate aircraft type with accompanying restrictions. Airplanes that are categorized as "heavy" are recognized for their wake-turbulence risk, so it requires additional spacing behind it to allow the wake to dissipate. This has created a safety margin that has worked well for many years now.

Another risk factor with regard to wake turbulence is aerodynamic efficiency. The more efficient a wing is, the more concentrated the wake it produces. When Boeing created the B-757, it didn't take long to discover that the ultra-efficient wing design produced a rather powerful wake. Even though the B-757 doesn't meet the weight criteria to be categorized as a "heavy" aircraft, it is treated like a "heavy" for wake-turbulence spacing purposes. Something that still escapes recognition is the wake produced by the B-737 which has a wing of similar efficiency to the B-757 and some of the latest versions are almost as big. The worst wake turbulence experiences I've encountered were following B-737s.

On the approach today, we suffered my worst tangle with wake turbulence. Troy was flying the airplane and the controller tucked us in just a couple miles behind a B-737. It started with a few bumps and then came the roll. The wake was rolling us hard left while Troy had the controls to the right. It stayed that way for a couple seconds and we were both pretty concerned for a moment. Fortunately, it didn't take very long to fly through it and Troy kept it under control, but it certainly confirmed again that B-737s generate a nasty wake. Considering my multiple encounters, I'm always a little extra cautious when following a B-737.

Captain's Log, Airdate 2000000

Breaking Loose

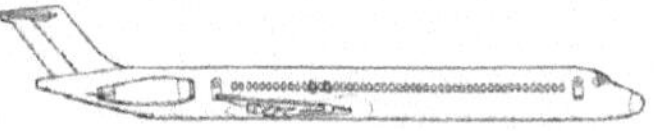

Aircraft: MD-80

The MD-80's two engines are mounted on the tail. These engines are the single heaviest components on the airplane, making it inherently tail heavy. As the aircraft is loaded with people, bags and fuel, the weight distribution is designed to even out and balance properly. We figure out the weight and balance point before every flight in order to verify this and ensure the machine will be controllable once it becomes airborne. The process is called a "weight and balance" calculation.

The dynamics of ground operations are different than in flight. The aircraft weight is supported by the wings while in the air but by the landing gear while on the ground. This difference changes the balance toward a tail-heavy tendency on the ground, which means a risk that the airplane could tip back on its tail. As long as we are moving forward with the engines running, this isn't a problem.

A concern arises, however, when we are moving *backwards.* In this case pilots are taught to use forward engine thrust to stop the airplane, *not* the brakes. The point of greatest exposure to this risk is when the tug is pushing us back from the gate: we are rolling backward with no engines running and the hydraulic steering disabled. This might seem a bit precarious, but the tug is attached to the nose gear, keeping it tethered to the ground, and as soon as an engine is running the risk is mostly mitigated.

As luck would have it, I happened to encounter the perfect storm of instability tonight. The pushback from the gate was downhill. As we began the push the tow bar broke loose, which left us rolling backward with no engines running and no steering. There were no appealing options at that point as we watched the tug crew get farther away and their expressions grow more concerned. I could attempt to start an engine in order to stop the backward movement, but this would take some time and I didn't know how close we were to the edge of the pavement. The best option was exactly what I didn't want to attempt: the brakes. I gently eased into the pedals to see if the nose would start to rise. It didn't! I then began a gradual process of easing a little bit more and assessing the nose with each successive increase. I was very grateful that it worked and we came to a stop. Crisis averted!

Captain's Log, Airdate 2000000

Ground Shift Relay

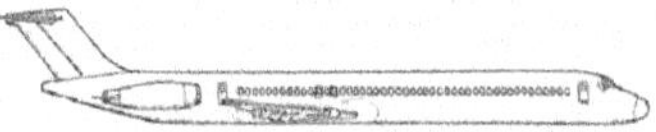

Aircraft: MD-80

Most pilots who fly the MD-80 are familiar with one of the most infamous accidents involving this airplane. SpanAir (a Spanish carrier) Flight 5022 crashed shortly after takeoff, killing everyone on board. The investigation revealed that the flaps were not set for takeoff, but it was the way they got there that is most instructive.

The flight initially began taxiing for takeoff with the flaps set correctly, but the crew discovered an instrumentation failure and chose to return to the gate. They retracted the flaps on the way back, as is typical for such a return. There is a probe on the nose of the airplane that provides temperature information for automatic engine thrust calculations. The temperature indication from this probe was way too high, so the crew could clearly see it was in error. Maintenance personnel agreed and they decided to "defer" fixing it until later. This is not uncommon and there are extensive rules about what is required in order to "defer" something. They dotted the i's and crossed the t's and got underway again with only a minimal delay. In their haste, however, they forgot to reset the flaps for takeoff on the second time around. It was a fatal error!

The flaps are essential for takeoff at normal speeds and thus are covered by a warning system that alerts the crew if they are not set correctly. This system also failed due to an anomaly that escaped detection. In reality, there was nothing wrong with the temperature probe. It was working exactly as it was designed to do—when it is *in the air*. The actual problem was a small electrical relay that senses whether the airplane is on the ground or in the air. This relay was sensing an airborne condition which caused the probe to be heated as it normally would be in flight to avoid ice accumulation. No one had realized this was the cause of the erroneous indications. More importantly, the system that warns of an incorrect flap setting was disabled because it "thought" it was already in the air.

Having learned from this accident, most MD-80 pilots are vigilant for the indications of a similar failure. The important aspect to look for is the function of the ground-shift relay. This small electrical component provides input for several aircraft systems to have a correct indication as to whether the airplane is airborne or not.

It happened to me on this flight. All indications were normal until we started the engines. I noticed the temperature indication was wrong, which led from one thing to another and ultimately the conclusion that the ground-shift relay was stuck in the airborne position. We eventually switched to a different airplane to allow for the faulty component to be changed. As we worked to prepare the next aircraft, the mechanics brought me the malfunctioning relay they had removed from the other plane. I couldn't help but reflect on the SpanAir accident as I held it in my hand. It was haunting to think of the role such a small component had played in such a huge tragedy.

On the Jump Seat

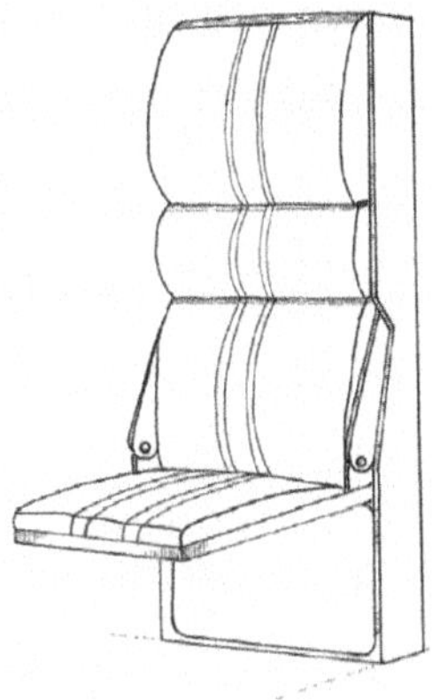

Travel benefits are one of the great perks that come with an airline job. Airline pilots can ride for free on just about any domestic carrier to destinations within the United States. A lot of international destinations are also available for just a small fee. This protocol has developed over the years as a professional courtesy between pilots: I let you ride on my aircraft if I can ride on yours. It's used most often to provide a means for pilots to travel from where they live to the airport where they are based to begin a trip and then travel home afterward. About half of airline pilots do not live where they are based. Even though any open seat on the airplane is available on any given flight, the practice is commonly known as jump-seating (referencing the jump seat in the flight deck). This practice is part of an airline's larger non-revenue (non-rev, for short) program available to all employees but the jump seat is only available to pilots, mechanics and dispatchers.

DEFINITION

Jump Seat:
An extra seat in the flight deck, behind the pilots. Some airplanes have two jump seats. Flight attendants also use jump seats in the cabin.

While this is a nice perk that comes with the job, it does have its challenges. A traveling pilot is never guaranteed a seat on a particular flight. If there are no seats available, the off-line pilot gets bumped and has to find a different way to get there. Sometimes even empty seats end up being unavailable for various reasons. Another nuisance is that most jump seats are not very comfortable, particularly the B-737 jump seats. The second jump seat on the B-737 is almost a medieval torture device.

Jump-seating is almost part of the job for an airline pilot and can be interesting, educational and even fun sometimes. I've met some fascinating people while riding on their jump seats or while they were riding on mine. Nearly all of us have done it at some point and some pilots do it all the time. I know a pilot who has never flown an MD-80 but has spent so much time on the jump seat that he knows practically everything about it just from watching. Overall, riding on the jump seat is usually a positive experience. The following section includes some memorable trips looking over the crew's shoulders.

Captain's Log, Airdate 140200

It's a Federal Aviation Regulation

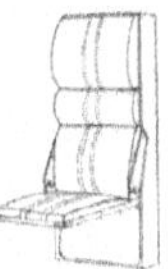

Aircraft: Jump Seat, Boeing 737

I was in New York and needed to get back home. Whenever I travel non-rev, I'm always cautious to make sure there are enough open seats, so I have some peace of mind that I won't get bumped. Paying passengers get priority over a non-rev traveler. When I planned this trip, there were over a hundred open seats between the three different carriers, so I wasn't concerned at all. My preferred airline was plan A because they always treated me so nicely. When I arrived at their ticket counter, however, I was informed that they had cancelled their flight. Uh oh! Not only was that flight no longer available, but those passengers would now roll into the remaining flights and, just like that, all the open seats were gone.

Now I was scrambling to find any way to get back home. I found a flight on another airline with an open jump seat and got on board.

Unfortunately, there was an unusually strong headwind that created a need for additional fuel and the aircraft would have been too heavy for takeoff. The captain apologized but had no choice other than to bump me off. I think even some paying passengers got displaced. I understood their predicament, so I quickly deplaned. It was becoming clear that I was not going to find a seat going where I wanted to, so I changed my strategy. My sister lived relatively close to Salt Lake City, Utah (SLC). While SLC was still a long way from home, it was a whole lot closer than where I currently stood. I called her and asked if I could spend the night at her house. I then found a flight to SLC with numerous open seats and said goodbye to New York.

After spending the night at my sister's house, I returned to SLC the next morning to resume my quest to find an open seat to get back home. It was a frustrating day with no success until mid-afternoon. The flight had more than 30 open seats. After more than 24 hours of strike outs, I had finally found what I was looking for. I approached the podium and politely asked if it was possible to get a seat. "No," was her quick response. It caught me off guard because I thought there were plenty of seats available, so I asked about it. She pointed out that there were open seats in the cabin, but the flight-deck jump seats were taken. Thinking she might have misunderstood, I told her a cabin seat was ok with me. Again, "No."

DEFINITION

Non-Rev:
The use of travel benefits rather than purchasing a ticket. It's free, but you have no assurance there will be a seat available.

I went back and forth with her several times to find some way to politely convince her to let me have one of those seats. She would not budge, because she claimed it was strictly against policy to take more than two jump-seat pilots. This was not true, but she was convinced she was right and seemed to be enjoying my torment. My frustration with her was building and blinding me to the obvious solution. Had I explained my situation to the two pilots who had beaten me to the jump-seats, they could have informed the captain of my plight and I'm confident he would have found a way to take care of me. I tried to play on her sympathy by sharing my story of frustration from the last 24 hours. She wasn't moved.

I finally asked, "Are you telling me there has never once been an exception to this policy?"

She said very seriously, "Oh, no! It's a *Federal Aviation Regulation*."

Not only was this absolutely false, but it was acutely irksome to hear her condescending tone about regulations. At this point I had reached the limit of my patience. Any further would have pushed me closer to a confrontation I might have regretted. I gave up on the battle! In the end, I did get a seat on the *next* flight, but was left with a permanent mistrust of the staff of that particular airline in SLC.

Captain's Log, Airdate 140700

Fifteen Minutes of Fame

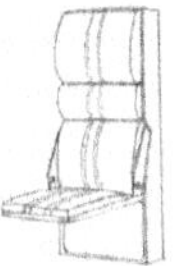

Aircraft: Jump Seat, Boeing 737

I was living in Tucson at this time and I was traveling to begin my upgrade training to become a captain on the MD-80. Upgrade training is a big deal and its considered proper to wear a suit when the time comes for the check ride. I was wearing my suit while jump-seating (very unusual) because it's easier to just wear it than to pack it and let it get all wrinkled in my bag. I happened to come across the first officer (FO) who was working the flight. He seemed like a nice guy and we started a short conversation. Eventually he asked about the suit, because it was so unusual. I explained my reasoning, but he still poked fun at me anyway.

After takeoff, the first officer decided to have more fun with me. He made his standard announcement to the passengers and then shifted to me:

"Also, ladies and gentlemen, we happen to have a celebrity on board with us today. I'm sure you all can recognize him—he's the only one wearing a suit. How 'bout if you raise your hand and wave?"

I decided to play along with his prank and I waved for my fellow passengers to identify me.

He went on, "He has been out of the country for a while doing stunt double work for Steven Seagal's latest movie. He normally travels by private jet but somehow ended up with us today." He embellished even further, and it was kind of funny, but I thought that would be the end of it.

After a few minutes, a flight attendant approached me and asked for my autograph. At first, I thought she was continuing the prank in cahoots with the first officer, but after a brief exchange and a look in her eyes, I realized she was serious. Now I didn't know how to proceed. In hindsight, it would have been better to just explain the whole thing right then, but she seemed like such a sweet girl and I couldn't figure out how to let her know without making her feel dumb. I tried to convince her that I was nobody and she really didn't want my autograph, but she was undeterred, thinking I was just being coy. After a couple of increasingly impassioned requests and my attempt to convince her that my autograph wasn't worth it, she upped the ante. She brought me every logo-branded knick-knack she could find (pen, pin, deck of cards, etc.) to cajole me. I gave in and scribbled something on a napkin to appease her.

I thought that would be the end of it, but we weren't done yet. As I was deplaning, she and the first officer were standing in the front together. No big deal, right? I could just slip past them and we would never see each other again. Oh no! As soon as the FO saw me, he started with the teasing again. Then he mentioned his announcement and asked if anybody was dumb enough to fall for that nonsense. Uh oh! I didn't know what to say. She was so embarrassed! She offered apologies, so I explained that I was trying to let her know that I was nobody important. She begged me to forget I had ever met her. I've never forgotten the moment and how sweet she was, but I couldn't even begin to remember what she looked like. I think she was blonde.

Captain's Log, Airdate 150318

Don't Be That Guy

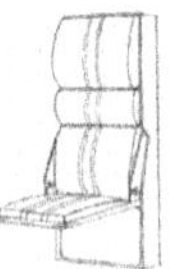

Aircraft: Jump Seat, MD-80

One of the biggest traps in the airline world is airports with similar runway layouts that are right next to each other. There are a few of these cases that involve Air Force Bases. Because the airports are so close to each other and the runways are so similar, the unsuspecting pilot can mistakenly land at the wrong one. Landing at a military field without prior authorization is big trouble. The solution to avoid getting caught in one of these traps is attention to detail and a high level of vigilance.

Tucson, Arizona (TUS) is just such an example. Davis-Monthan AFB (DMA) is located right next door with a runway nearly identical to its neighbor. Compounding the difficulty in this case was the crew's lack of familiarity plus the fact that it was after dark. With nothing but a sea of lights around them, it was more challenging to identify the correct lights. I watched as the crew set up the approach exactly as they should have, but the captain then began maneuvering toward DMA. I could see what was happening and I would certainly not have allowed them to follow through on such a big mistake. I had a responsibility on the jump seat as a third set of eyes. What intrigued me in this case was that the first officer (FO) voiced his concern that something wasn't right, but the captain was undeterred. With his input rebuffed, the FO was intently looking through his charts to ensure he was right before he brought it up again.

A few moments passed and it was about time for me to say something, but the captain finally realized his mistake. What happened next is what made such a memorable impression on me. The captain started to chide the FO for not correcting him. I felt like smacking the guy. The FO had indeed said something, although lacking specifics, and he got shut down. He was in the process of building a more convincing case when the captain finally oriented himself. Rather than listening to the FO in the first place, he continued stubbornly and then blamed *him* after he had tried to help.

Advice to every captain: Don't be that guy.

Captain's Log, Airdate 210321

Ghost Rider in the Sky

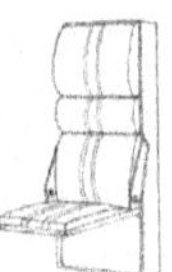

Aircraft: Jump Seat, Boeing 757

I had taken a temporary assignment in Chicago, Illinois (ORD) that had me commuting home on the weekends. The return back to ORD was always crowded, so I had to plan multiple options in case I got bumped. As a pilot, I can usually ride on the flight deck jump seat, which offers an extra option when the airplane is full. A nationwide system has been established in order to verify pilot credentials for admittance to the flight deck. On this particular day, that system wasn't working. This meant serious trouble. It was unlikely that I would find an open seat in the cabin on any airline that day. I had no choice but to hang around and hope that the system would resume normal operations at some point.

As I waited, something strange happened. My first choice of the flights available was with a very large U.S. carrier. This company employs thousands of flight attendants and I happened to know exactly *one* of them. I hadn't seen her for years and I had been wondering just that weekend how she was doing. She happened to be working that very flight. When we saw each other, we immediately began catching up. She asked what I was doing and I explained my current situation. She then offered to talk to the captain on my behalf. With her vouching for me, he decided to allow me on the flight deck. This is absolutely unheard of. He was sticking his neck out for a stranger. I was amazed and grateful that the situation had worked out.

I boarded the airplane and settled into the jump seat. As departure time approached, the gate agent came to the captain and requested information for the jump-seater. The captain asked, “What jump-seater?” Again I was impressed and grateful. The gate agent again tried to get my information, but the captain replied, “He’s not here.” The agent then decided to defer to the captain and let it go. To me it was miraculous that the situation had worked out somehow when there was no apparent solution available.

Captain's Log, Airdate 270800

We'll Just Wait

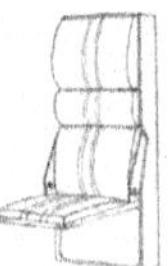

Aircraft: Jump Seat, Boeing 737

Airline flying is amazingly safe. In fact, it's statistically safer than riding in a car. Millions of people every day board airlines throughout the world and arrive safely to their destinations. Evidence of this can be found everywhere, but the majority of flyers don't give much thought to its significance. Flying is not only one of the safest forms of travel, but we are also currently enjoying a "golden age" with regard to avoiding accidents. Nevertheless, there is obvious risk associated with lifting ourselves into the air and flying thousands of feet above the ground at hundreds of miles per hour in a pressurized tube. This is what most people think of when it comes to the fear of flying—the part that's in the air.

What escapes the awareness of the masses is the risks we face on the ground. As a veteran pilot, this is where I am most attuned to the risk factors around me, especially when it comes to runways. Runway incursions (incidents that involve aircraft getting too close to any type of collision risk on takeoff or landing) are serious business. Runways are like busy streets. Crossing them is not to be taken casually and requires the highest attention level. Not only does the "look both ways" principle apply, but listening carefully to radio transmissions gives vital information as to the status of a runway. On takeoff or landing, the shoe is on the other foot: the crew must carefully watch and listen for other aircraft or vehicles that might enter the runway at the wrong moment.

Great efforts have been put into runway safety for many years now and the fruits of those efforts have yielded a number of benefits. One of the most important innovations in this regard is the Runway Status Light System. Most large airports are now equipped with this valuable installation that is as simple to use as a traffic light—red means stop. It uses radar to monitor runway collision threats and activates the red lights if anything is detected inside the boundary. It's an amazing enhancement that adds one more layer of safety to pilot and controller vigilance.

While I've never seen the system malfunction, I've always wondered just how trustworthy it is. Today I was thoroughly impressed. I wear a headset for most of my flights on the jump seat and I'm glad I did in this case. We had just landed and were taxiing to the terminal when we heard an unusual exchange on the radio. The tower cleared someone for takeoff, but he rejected the clearance because the red lights were indicating it wasn't safe. The system had detected an airplane on final approach. At that point, dozens of eyes turned that direction to see what the radar was detecting. What we saw was a small airplane that had somehow slipped through the cracks. It was a strong reinforcement for me as to the reliability and usefulness of that system. It can't ever replace human vigilance, but it's ingenious and innovative and I'm grateful that it has been so widely implemented so we can all reap the benefits of enhanced runway safety.

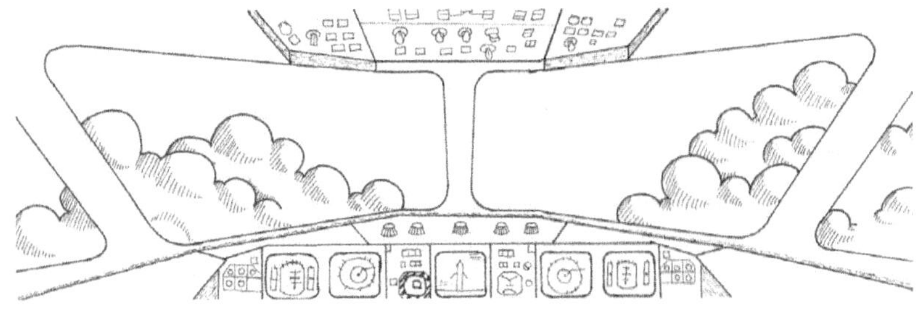

Looking Forward

Looking back on my flying memories from the last 30 years has been quite an experience. Capturing some of these stories in writing has been a labor of love that I hope you have found enjoyable and enlightening. I truly believe I have the best part-time job in the world. I wouldn't want to trade it for any other. I realize I will eventually be dragged away from it kicking and screaming someday, but I intend to enjoy what I can until then.

If you are among those who enjoy aviation and its benefits as a passenger or enthusiast, I hope my stories have been interesting and educational. I hope you have a new-found appreciation for, and understanding of, what goes on behind the flight deck door. What we do can certainly seem mysterious and amazing. I have heard frequent comments about all the buttons and switches that surround us in the flight deck and many of us quip that we know what "some of them" do. Operating big jets safely is definitely complex and demanding but amazingly simple at the same time. I once heard a captain sum it all up in a preflight briefing like this, "Just don't hit anything."

If you might be considering a career in aviation, I highly recommend it. We live in a time of tremendous opportunity for those with the courage and commitment to take on the challenge and put in the effort to prepare themselves. It takes work, but it's not rocket science. The dividends from the investment have been worth it for me and many of my good friends. I would hope for many of the same rewards for you as well.

My love affair with flying has been just a small sliver of the much larger world of airborne adventures. Since Orville and Wilbur Wright first "slipped the surly bonds of earth," aviators have enjoyed the challenges of taming the skies one flight at a time, one airplane at a time, one generation at a time. As my generation passes into history, a new one will continue to write the saga of mankind's journey through the atmosphere and beyond our terrestrial home. The invitation to help write the story is extended to anyone willing to make the effort. Come join us!